The
Bible

A PACK OF LIES—
OR
GOD'S HONEST TRUTH?

DD RENFROE

PARADIGM LIGHTHOUSE

ISBN: 979-8-9924788-2-2 paperback; 979-8-9924788-3-9 ebook.

Library of Congress Control Number 2025920636

Published in the United States of America by Paradigm Lighthouse Ministries, 56 Woodwind Way, Freeport FL 32439

ParadigmLighthouse.com

WHAT READERS ARE SAYING

Excerpts of praise by everyday people:

- Well worth the wait! Hard to put down! The author is brilliant....*Chris H.*
- A meticulous scholar and effective communicator... *Barbara J.*
- Extensive research and dedication.... *Gerald M.*
- An epic story of survival.... *Denise G.*
- The kind of book you return to over and over as your Bible reading raises new questions.... *Barbara J.*
- Easy-to-read unveiling.... *Brit F.*
- An excellent by-the-numbers exploration of God's Revelation.... *Bruce K.*
- Very enjoyable....*Jeff E.*
- Proves that the Bible isn't like any other book..... *Lisa F.*
- A cornucopia of fascinating historical facts and biblical truths that further affirm the validity of the world's favorite book..... *Henry H.*
- A great read.... *Micah S.*
- Adding to my classroom list of further reading recommendations.... *Allison W.*
- A panoramic view of the history of the Bible.... *David G.*
- Such an important, thorough, simple work....*Jim T.*
- Satisfies an educated reader who wants an overview.... *Andrew W.*
- Eye-opening to the sincere dedication demonstrated by countless believers.... *Rebecca P.*
- Well-written, interesting and provides solid information for answering the question: "Why should I believe the Bible?" *Sally S.*
- Just two chapters into this book, I was like WOW! *Grover S.*

Everyone's full comments can be seen at paradigmlighthouse.com. The endorsements of pastors, authors and influencers continue after the Bibliography.

CONTENTS

INTRODUCTION

I love a good mystery! One I can watch, hear, or read anytime—as long as it's not salacious, overly graphic, or cruel.

Who dun' it? Why?

This book started in 2016 as my own investigation into the sources of Scripture, just for fun. As I spent more and more time and money—books, old magazines, museums, travel, and the like—this hobby became a passion, even I daresay an addiction.

If only other people knew how authoritative, authentic, and even real Scripture is, maybe they would come out of our cultural shell and explore it for themselves.

That is my hope for you, dear reader, and especially for those discouraged by militant anti-Bible professors and teachers. I knew several in grad school in my forties. I was less vulnerable at my age but saw the destruction of faith in my younger friends.

I pray that this book enriches your life, no matter where you fall on the scale of Scripture knowledge. A person can say, "I don't believe the Bible," but they can't say, "It's not real."

As you will see...

D D Renfroe

May 2025

CHAPTER 1

THE BEGINNING

THE SCRIPTURE OF THE HEART, HELD IN MEMORY

BEFORE THERE WAS WRITING, THERE WAS MEMORY—AND POWERFUL memory it was. This kind of memory was not at all like the gossip game, in which a word whispered from person to person is unrecognizable by the time it returns to the first in line.

Instead, this was **ethnic memory** which transcends individual memory and time. Memory before writing was a life force for preliterate cultures, and it is still for the few remaining non-literate ones. All of their history, survival strategies, ancestry, and more depended on memory—not just individual memory but tribal memory and group memory, all passed from to generation to generation with remarkable accuracy. Indeed, the book of Genesis in Scripture reveals hints of an oral preliterate culture, and a window into its collective, generational memory from Adam and Eve to Moses.

STUDIES AND HINTS

What do studies show about tribal memory, past and current? Some research such as Dr. Lynne Kelly's *The Memory Code* shows that in the absence of writing, ethnic groups rely on **trusted elder group members and memory ceremonies**. This enables the tribe to save and transmit important history and knowledge to successive generations of their people. Along with singing and dancing, mnemonic devices (memory aids) included star patterns, outdoor spaces, drawings and carvings on wood or stone. Such traditions preserve memory profoundly which endures for many generations, much like our ABC song today. (I can still recite verbatim the Crest toothpaste commercial from the sixties.) In addition, if a member of the tribal group went rogue from the known pattern, they could be quickly corrected, and if needed, forcibly. It was that important.

THE HISTORY-STAFF

The ethnic memory was obviously transmitted through the generations of mankind somehow, and in some durable way. Transmission to the Israelite generations came into the Bible, while differing versions of Creation and the Flood were passed down in other cultures, with far less profundity and accuracy.

Throughout human history, **wood staffs** have played a natural part in multiple ways which are seen in Scripture. Staffs had that durable quality, plus the versatility of usefulness. They play a repeated role in the book of Genesis, and throughout biblical history.

Perfectly portable and lasting, staffs were useful for walking and herding, for self-defense, and for religion. Such staffs likely preserved stories through their carvings. A person might think of totem poles in northwest America as story-telling staffs.

In light of this proven history, I have **my theory** about how the history of Creation and the human race would have come into the Bible. Imagine with me the weighty village meetings of the early families descended from Adam and Eve in the young, wild world.

They hold the ceremonial hardwood staffs, whose carvings depict the events important to rehearse and pass down faithfully without embellishment. Someone recites the history in the hearing of all; perhaps someone sings and dances as well to portray the drama and feelings in their group saga.

Trusted elders were the pillars of ancient societies; such leaders would enforce fidelity to the received knowledge with a methodical transmission of the meaning of the carvings. Anyone who embellishes or deviates from the accepted retelling will be corrected or denied the honor to be a re-teller. After the event or ceremony, elders gather the master staffs for the next time; perhaps one elder is charged to curate them until he is succeeded by the next elder.

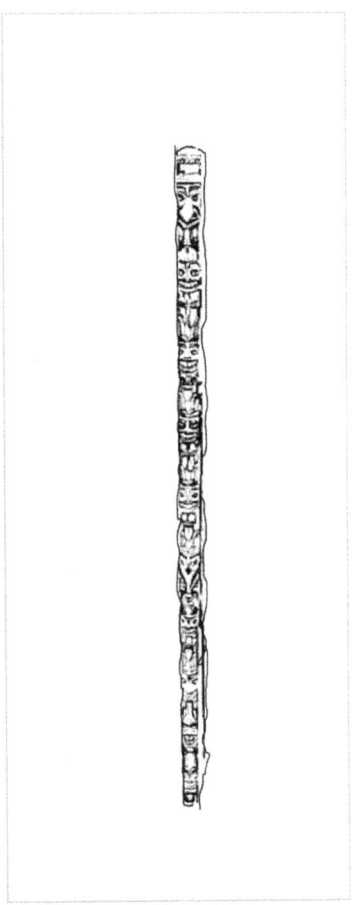

Staff showing mnemonic carvings (artist unknown).

By many such groups with their staff collections, an undisrupted transference of their ethnic and spiritual history is assured. When a staff is lost, destroyed, or wears out, someone can replace these staffs fairly easily, with new ones bearing the same stories in carvings.

My theory about the history staffs is an educated guess, well-founded on God's proven longing to make Himself known to people. The pattern is proven in other non-literate cultures of the past. It supports the idea that such mnemonic tools could, and likely did, transmit revelation faithfully about our creation and our fall.

Is there biblical evidence of such mnemonic staffs? Several Scriptures are best explained by the existence of carved staffs telling their tale.

In the Torah, Numbers 17:1–11 hints at this device of carved history staffs. Their use is also implied negatively, in connection with idolatry.

Write the name of each man on his staff. On the staff of Levi write Aaron's name, for there must be one staff for the head of each ancestral tribe. (Numbers 17:2–3)

My people ask counsel from their wooden idols,
And their staff informs them. (Hosea 4:12 NKJV)

Noah, a major elder, was a preacher of righteousness (see 2 Peter 2:5) when the Flood came, an event which only he and his family survived. If these mnemonic staffs of history existed, Noah would preserve a collection (or several collections) aboard the ark. After the Flood, they would add the recent events to a new staff.

Noah's Ark (You can visit the full-size replica at the Ark Encounter in Williamstown, Kentucky.)

THEN CAME WRITING

Vital to the production of Scripture is the development of writing— but how, when, and where? The modern sense of invention does not apply to writing; rather, it developed over time—first out of economic necessity, perhaps recording caravan deliveries and inventory. The Scripture began to be composed in the civilizations which arose in the Fertile Crescent, on both the eastern and western sides. Each developed very different writing forms starting in about 3200 to 3400 BC, or even earlier.

On the **eastern side** of Mesopotamia, the civilization of Sumer was so incredibly advanced that more adventuresome thinkers propose aliens taught them. Sumerians used a type of writing we call *cuneiform*. Scribes pressed wedge-shaped marks onto wet clay tablets which were then dried in the sun, making them extremely durable, many lasting even to this day.

Vast libraries of clay tablets uncovered in Sumer have yielded a wealth of knowledge about the business, worship, and lifestyles of that most ancient culture. The Sumerian city Ur of the Chaldees was the home from which God called Abram (later Abraham), God's first recorded friend.

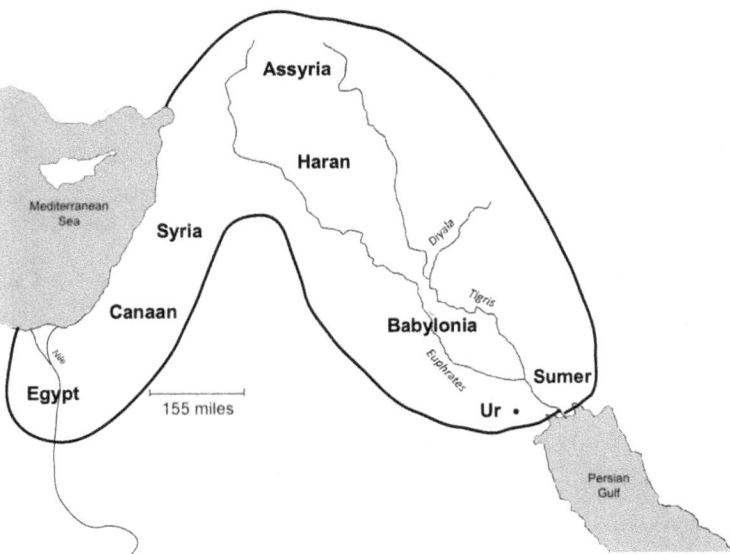

Fertile Crescent with major regional names.

From what was Abraham called? According to cuneiform and archeological evidence, Sumer was a thoroughly pagan society, steeped in astrological worship using sexual practices at ziggurats. Sumer offered its inhabitants some safety from attack, great wealth, and the intellectual pursuits of the time. Abram and Sarai's attachment to Ur, its comforts, and its people would naturally be strong, but the call of God was stronger. God called Abram, a Semitic man, from the Sumerians who had a written language—and thus He laid the foundation for a people to compose the Scripture.

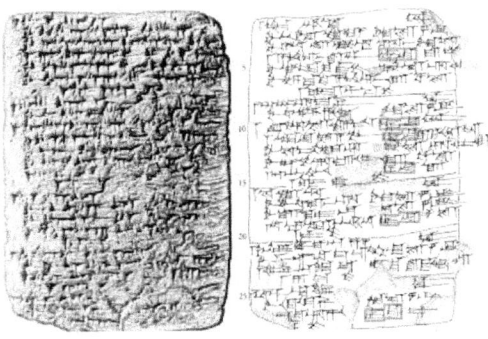

Cuneiform tablet with line replica. (Bartosz Bogatz, Michael Gertz, and Hupert Mara. "Cuneiform Character Similarity Using Graph Representations," Heidelberg University, Germany, 2015. https://d-nb. info/1191851303/34)

Over on the **western side** of the Fertile Crescent, the Egyptians developed pictographic figures of trading products on coin-like ostraca, shards of broken pottery (their version of Post-It notes!), preserved in jars. They also developed a quick everyday writing script, called *hieratic*, while using the ceremonial hieroglyphics of the pharaohs familiar to us from their tombs and other records intended to be permanent.

For Egypt, as for Sumer, their gift of writing was a setup for the Scripture, which that amazing civilization could barely have imagined. From pictographs and their everyday script on ostraca to the more advanced hieroglyphics we see today on the walls of pharaohs' tombs, the Egyptians continued to advance in writing skills while using a variety of materials. Egyptian scribes were products of the **best writing schools** in the world. All this seems arranged to occur in the home country of the young man Moses.

Hieratic script (L) beside hieroglyphs (R). (Catherine Paganini. "Hieroglyphs 101: An Introduction to the Language of the Pharaohs," 2021. https://www.linkedin.com/pulse/hieroglyphs-101-introduction-language-pharaohs-catherine-paganini)

MOSES: THE MAN, THE WAY, THE RIGHT TIME

Moses—what a person! What a life! Who could have been more qualified? Moses both led the Children of Israel out of Egyptian slavery and wrote their history. It wasn't only their national history, but their history with the God they were coming to know and call their own.

Moses was the son of Hebrew slaves, saved from certain death when a pharaoh, fearful of the Hebrews' high birthrate, ordered the killing of all male Hebrew babies. Amid this mass genocidal infanticide, a pharaoh's daughter found Moses in a river and adopted him. Raised in the palace with all the advantages of Egyptian royalty, he was in the upper echelon of Egyptian life. (See Exodus 2:1–8.)

While in Egypt, Moses would have received a royal education widely known to be the best in their world. This schooling surely included the art of writing and the young Moses may have had a special affinity for writing, as his later work in the Sinai desert attests.

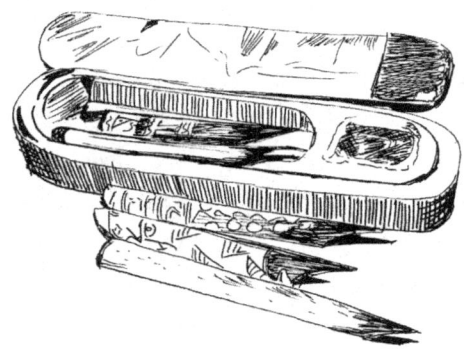

Egyptian reed pen from the Roman period. (Image courtesy of the British Museum; sketch by artist Katie Dale.)

Yet he was evidently deeply connected to his Hebrew background as well—and a hothead to boot in his early years. When the daughter of the pharaoh needed a nurse for the unweaned baby Moses, his own mother was chosen (see Exodus 2:9–10). The values thus nurtured in him burst forth violently when he witnessed and killed an Egyptian slave-master beating a fellow Hebrew (see Exodus 2:11–14).

> By faith Moses, when he had grown up, refused to be known as the son
> of Pharaoh's daughter. He chose to be mistreated along with the people
> of God... (Hebrews 11:24–25)

To avoid the death penalty for killing a slave master, Moses left Egypt and his luxurious life (see Exodus 2:15). Thus began **the rest of his preparation** in a backwoods place called Midian, far from the reach of the Egyptians, which plausibly he may have scouted for the future. There he married a shepherdess and joined the family business for forty years (see Exodus 2:16–22).

Becoming a father and shepherd provided good training for leading people, as King David demonstrated centuries later. And Moses had time to reflect upon his actions in Egypt while he still longed to help his people and serve his God.

Indeed, he must have led a physically vigorous life to prepare him for the next forty years—leading the Hebrews through the same or similar wildernesses.

His time in Midian ended when Moses heard the voice of God calling him from a bush, curiously burning but not consumed. That bush was the first of an amazing string of recorded miracles, the likes of which are rarely seen—miracles which culminated in the eventual release of the Israelites into the wilderness heading for the Promised Land.

Now in this wilderness, Moses assembled **a crew of scribes**. Writing alone, like Nathaniel Hawthorne in his tiny attic, was an act thousands of years in the future. In ancient culture, writing was a group endeavor.

Thus Moses began his most lasting pursuit—writing and collecting God's very words, recording them for posterity. He was now about eighty years old. Did he know these writings would stand the test of time so much that they **live today all over the world**—when only fragments of other writings in those days still exist? Did he know that his precious people would become known as the People of the Book?

HOW DID MOSES KNOW?

Early in his sojourn in the wilderness with the Israelites, Moses received the Ten Commandments written by the hand of God on stone—can you imagine!? Upon his unfortunate encounter with Aaron's golden calf, Moses broke the stone tablets. He next received a copy from God to replace the broken originals; this pair was preserved in the Ark of the Covenant (see Exodus 25:16). **These events set writing in motion** for the Children of Israel.

Moses next received much more instruction from God than can fit on stone. And so it became a **writing assignment** which set the precedent for millennia to this day.

> Then the LORD said to Moses, "Write this on a scroll as something to be remembered and make sure Joshua hears it." (Exodus 17:14)

> So Moses wrote down this law and gave it to the Levitical priests, who carried the ark of the covenant of the Lord, and to all the elders of Israel. (Deuteronomy 31:9)

THE SCROLL

Moses needed **writing material**, and he didn't have to look far. Egypt had developed a well-suited set of materials perfect for writing and even toting around the desert: papyrus, carbon ink, and brush reeds for pens. They made papyrus by laying out the fibers of the reeds which grew abundantly in the area and processing them into a thin, absorbent, paper-like material. Workers next glued (or sewed) the pieces together and rolled them up, making about a thirty-four-foot scroll or shorter.

Add a dowel on each end, and the scroll was ready for the carbon-based ink, which was also widely available. Writers applied ink with a reed cut into a kind of brush. Now Moses had readily available, perfectly portable, desert-friendly material with which to begin his divinely commanded project. How handy!

ENTER THE SCRIBES

In the company of the newly freed Israelites were many skilled workers, mentioned at least eight times when it was time to build the Tabernacle (see Exodus 28:3, for example). The Egyptians had probably trained these artisans as slaves for work in their culture.

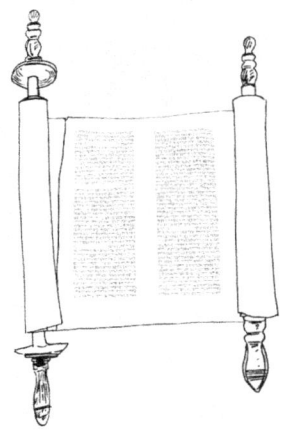

Drawing of a Torah scroll. (Sketch by artist Katie Dale.)

From the biblical record, this group included skilled scribes and the tribe of Levites, newly minted into service. As was customary in antiquity, entire clans would serve as scribes for generations (see 1 Chronicles 2:55). Along with many other duties, these workers were prophetically charged to help future kings know the Law and keep it before the people.

> When he [a king in Israel] takes the throne of his kingdom, he is to write for himself on a scroll a copy of this law, taken from that of the Levitical priests. It is to be with him, and he is to read it all the days of his life.... (Deuteronomy 17:18–19, insert added))

The first Egyptian-trained Israelite scribes, who probably assisted the leaders in the Israelite exodus, had seen the miracles and been witnesses to the awe of Mount Sinai. To say that fear and awe made them **more faithful** to their tasks is not a leap. All of these witnesses helped develop the reverence for the Scripture that lasts to this day.

A posse of scribes helping Moses record the Sinai revelation for posterity. (Image generated by ChatGPT, OpenAI, 2025.)

In addition, these scribes may also have trained the Levites in scribal arts. Until Jesus' time, scribes are little mentioned in Scripture. However, many books are named which aren't preserved today, such as the Book of Jasher, in Joshua 10:3 and 2 Samuel 1:18. The Book of the Wars of the LORD is another example, in Numbers 21:14. Scribes were the laborers who recorded and produced copies of these books now lost to history.

They were the hidden heroes of their day, who affect us still. Enigmatic and quiet, their work product speaks of their **meticulous dedication and devout care**. In his day, Moses himself surely needed their help with the two major censuses recorded in Numbers—not to mention the daily administrative tasks of governing nearly two million Israelites, requiring thousands of documents.

Like other writers of his day, Moses would have a crew—or a posse—of these important servants. He did not sit alone in a tent and write all day. Such scribes for the Bible continued until the advent of the printing press in the AD 1440s.

WHAT LANGUAGE?

The first five books of the Old Testament are called the Law of Moses, and also the Pentateuch. What language did Moses use to write them? This remains a mystery to this day. We can put together a few ideas from what we know.

One might suppose Egyptian to be the language, but this is unlikely. Several factors show that the Egyptians and Hebrews remained separate socially and physically, except for slave activities.

Hebrew men were bearded and engaged in manual labor and shepherding. In contrast, the Egyptians look bathed, had meticulous hairstyles, and used face makeup. The name "Hebrew," which the Egyptians called the Israelites, was a derogatory term meaning dusty ones. The Israelites called themselves the Children of Israel. Many of them lived separately in Goshen—shepherding livestock, living a pastoral lifestyle, and forging their identity as a people separate from the Egyptians.

Both cultures needed to be bilingual to some degree in order to conduct the business of the area. Slave and ghetto cultures typically develop pidgin languages to communicate with speakers of the dominant language, grammatically simplified with a limited number of words from both. Speakers of the two languages can communicate about simple matters. Additionally, some became fluent in Egyptian; others semi-fluent; and some knowing little if any.

If Hebrew were a written language in about 1400 BC, Moses would have used it (called *proto-Hebrew* by linguists today). But whatever the language of the first ink-to-papyrus Scripture, the Israelites—standing to listen—understood the Law when Moses read it aloud to them (see Exodus 24:7). Indeed at his death they had a copy they could read to their children and hand down (see Deuteronomy 31:11–13).

MORE EVIDENCE FOR MOSES' AUTHORSHIP

Tradition is and was a forceful element of the Jewish life—both written and orally transmitted. No one, even in Jesus' day, disputed Moses' authorship of the Law; Jesus affirmed it. The written testimonials of eyewitnesses and participants were trusted for thousands of years. Such a life-giving tradition carried the people of God through the rough life they faced. And because of the record written by Moses, the Children of Israel had a more secure basis for their belief in God. Truly, they were and still are the People of the Book.

In addition, Jesus Himself attests to Moses' authorship of the Law, which is evident often throughout the New Testament. Here are but a few:

> "What did Moses command you?" he [Jesus] replied. They said, "Moses permitted a man to write a certificate of divorce and send her away." "It was because your hearts were hard that Moses wrote you this law," Jesus replied. (Mark 10:3–5, insert added)

> But do not think I will accuse you before the Father. Your accuser is Moses, on whom your hopes are set. If you believed Moses, you would believe me, for he wrote about me. (John 5:45–46)

> Now about the dead rising—have you not read in the Book of Moses, in the account of the burning bush, how God said to him, "I am the God of Abraham, the God of Isaac, and the God of Jacob"? (Mark 12:26)

As a **Book which foreshadowed Jesus**, the Old Testament expanded to include the testimony of His eyewitnesses and was entrusted to the care of His followers since the first century AD.

FROM ARTIFACT TO CONTENT

How did Moses know? From Exodus onward, Moses is the subject or **the eyewitness** to all he wrote. But what about Genesis? How did he know about Creation, the Flood, and the rest? Many biblical researchers have attempted to answer this question, which Moses never answers. We have previously looked at the power and endurance of cultural oral history and mnemonic devices such as carved wooden staffs, so that is one theory among several.

DIVINE REVELATION

I like the way Dr. Bill Hamon says it in his 2005 book, *Who Am I and Why Am I Here*:

> How did Moses know the accurate details of heaven and earth and mankind? In modern terminology we would probably say that God showed Moses a video playback of the whole thing [can you imagine?!]

while he was on Mount Sinai with God for 40 days and nights. However, I think [Moses went] back in time and space before time began. He was privileged to see the unfolding of earth and mankind. He saw the past just as in the New Testament Apostle John was taken into the timeless dimension of Heaven and shown the future of mankind.

Considering the prevalence of divine revelation, prophecy, and miracles in Moses' time, the above explanation is completely plausible. At the very least, all the events prior to the creation of people could only be known by revelation.

So, why should we look further for any other theories? Well, because exploring plausible explanations is compelling. Just as the Bible is full of supernatural revelation, so it is filled with writing from both oral and written sources. So, a careful look at some other sources is helpful to our journey, as long as they don't violate the integrity of Scripture.

THE TOLEDOTH THEORY

The question that sparked this theory comes from Genesis because the list of generations there has an odd order. A phrase meaning "these are the generations of" (called *toledoth* in Hebrew) comes after, not before, the list associated with this name.

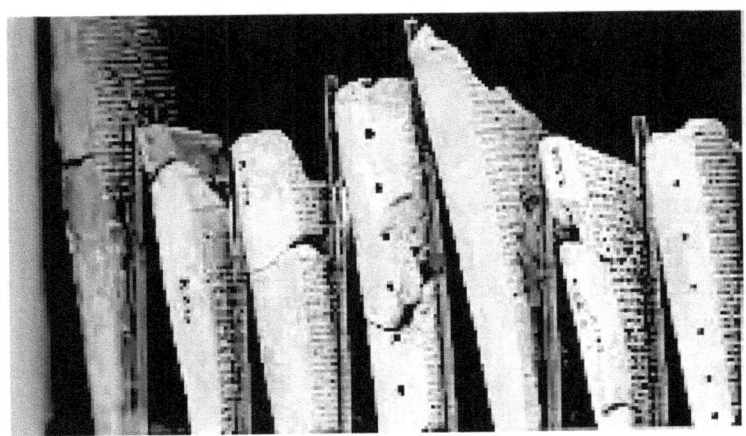

Clay tablets with colophon edges, shelved in a sample library setting.
(Photograph by Hannah Olson from the British Museum.)

Biblical researchers saw that in the libraries of Sumer, many thousands of stored clay tablets had a short title for cataloguing inscribed on the tablet's side.

These short titles, called colophons, enabled easy storage and retrieval. Colophons gave the subject and a brief description of the tablet's contents on its side—just as libraries store books so you can see the spine with the title, author, and shelving code in the Dewey decimal system.

Is this cataloging related to the Genesis order? Could "these are the generations of Jacob" be a colophon, a toledoth describing the contents of a clay tablet? Could such a tablet with such a list have been passed down to Moses eventually? If so, Moses would use them to help him compose Genesis in part or the whole. Using **genuine sources** does not violate the integrity of Scripture.

If Moses did have such a library of tablets for the history preceding the Exodus, how did he get them? Maybe Abram wrote, or had scribes write, the oral history of his Semitic people before leaving the Sumerian city of Ur. Plausibly, Abram took a chest of his family library with him and passed them down to Moses through Isaac, Jacob, and the twelve tribes.

There is no proof of this ancient possibility; the intriguing idea might explain the puzzling way the generations are presented in Genesis. If true, this means oral history was put in writing much earlier than previously supposed. We do not have definitive answers, so ancient and dim are the subjects of this investigation.

IN THE END

Excluding the events preceding Moses' lifetime, the Pentateuch comes from eyewitness accounts of Moses and his extensive conversations with God. As to the sources of Genesis, really all we have are faint, but intriguing, echoes from ancient times. A combination of memory staffs, oral history, written history, and divine revelation comes closest to explaining Moses' sources for Genesis. He did not say, and Scripture does not say.

But the **result was the first five books of the Bible**, called the Torah and also the Pentateuch, which were so heavily cited in both Old and New Testaments—and that was enough for God's chosen to know Him.

PRESENTATION

How was the Law, the Scripture, presented to the people? The Israelites heard the very voice of God from Mount Sinai, and it so scared them they begged Moses to make it stop. Instead, they wanted Moses to speak God's words to them secondhand. From then on, **the Law was read aloud to the people who stood**

in assembly, a tradition that continues to this day in churches and synagogues. If you are in a church and stand for the reading of the Bible, you are participating in a very ancient ritual and sign of respect.

The Tabernacle in the camp (image by Collectie Nederland). (Michael M. Homan. "The Tabernacle in Its Ancient Near Eastern Context." TheTorah.com, 2023. https://www.thetorah.com/article/the-tabernacle-in-its-ancient-near-eastern-context)

Only a few in those early days could read. Indeed, only Moses and some priests and scribes had the privilege of reading for themselves. So, the Scripture as it began was written, followed, memorized, and read to the Israelites. They then lived, treasured, protected, and loved the Torah beyond any book before or since. It provided not only their religion but also their government and daily guide for living.

So began the production, content, and presentation of Scripture. Lasting traditions were set for the writing and collecting of information for future Scripture—eyewitness accounts, written sources, and divine revelation. The means of presentation were set—oral reading to the people by a literate leader, with private reading a rare privilege until written material became common in the distant future.

As time passed, the original documents began to wear, and it's good they did. If we still had the original scroll of the Law, we would probably worship it and fight over it. In its place, a tradition of disposal began. Indeed, who could just trash or burn such a treasure? So, the tradition of carefully burying or reverently disposing of used Scripture began, along with the process of saving the Scripture through **reverent, meticulous copying** onto new scrolls. In such a copying process, no alterations would be tolerated, just as oral memory had allowed no wandering.

The Israelites now had a reliable history; it contained not just their earthly history as a people, but their interaction with YHWH who was their God. From all this, they could discern His character and know who it was they worshiped. **God stood in sharp contrast** to the demonic gods of the surrounding cultures and their detestable required practices: child sacrifice, infanticide, prostitution, and murder.

THE LAST PICTURE

As for Moses—what with Aaron his brother claiming the golden calf just popped out of the fire: what with the rebellion of Korah, he and his family screaming as the earth opened and closed around them and their possessions— what with the constant complaints, rebellions, and demands of the Israelites ("Water! Meat! Back to Egypt!")—well, though he loved his people, Moses may have been glad to be relieved of them.

You could say he lived agony and ecstasy—from the plagues of Egypt to the exodus from Pharaoh, from Mount Sinai to the golden calf, from *shekinah* glory to striking the rock. With all these highs and lows, Moses may have been glad to lay down this mortal coil and go with God—until, of course, he returns for a chat with Jesus and Elijah on the Mount of Transfiguration (see Matthew 17:3).

The last chapter of Deuteronomy records how God showed Moses the Promised Land from afar. Then his death is recorded either by Joshua or one of Moses' crew—or even prophetically by Moses (again not violating the integrity of Scripture). He was probably one hundred twenty years old at the time his amazing life ended. And in the end, he had what we all wish for—great stamina and clear eyesight!

THE CROSSING

What a wonderful, profound sight it must have been, after all their wandering, to see the Israelites crossing the Jordan into the Promised Land!

Well organized, well led, determined, all flags flying—even crossing the Jordan on dry land once again, as they had crossed the Red Sea in their exodus forty years earlier!

Today, that pageantry is gone, all but one item which rode (or was carried) right next to the Ark of the Covenant—the Torah, the incipient Bible. Later it would be placed beside the Ark in the Tabernacle.

Perhaps the Levites and Moses knew its infinite value, but how could they know those new scrolls would outlive the rise and fall of multiple civilizations for thousands of years?

Torah in the Ark, crossing the Jordan. (Sketch by artist Katie Dale.)

How could they know that the number of these new scrolls would multiply and become known as *a living and active double-edged sword* (Hebrews 4:12)? They could never have guessed their scrolls would reveal the Lord Jesus Christ to billions of people across the world over the centuries!

CHAPTER 2

JOSHUA TO JESUS

SOME LIGHT, SOME DARKNESS

WE NOW ENTER A PERIOD OF ANCIENT BIBLICAL HISTORY DURING which, outside Scripture itself, little is known about its formation, preservation, and presentation. Whereas the earlier civilizations of Sumer and Egypt left many well-preserved records in cuneiform and hieroglyphics, far fewer records remain from the Canaanite civilization toward which the Israelites marched.

The Israelites' wilderness wanderings and life in their Promised Land created very few permanent records for archaeologists to discover. The evidence that remains is their living Book itself.

The early alphabets were pictographic. The roots of our symbolic alphabet were actually in Canaan, thanks to the trading prowess of the Phoenician society, yet none of their written invoices and bills of lading survive. This is not unexpected; written records using permanent materials were unique to Sumer and Egypt. Writing intended for preservation was on stone inscriptions such as memorials. All else succumbed quickly to desert conditions.

For example, a *stele* (a large stone tablet) was unearthed in 1993 bearing the inscribed name of King David; it was named for the place of its discovery, Tel Dan. In 2024, a highly artistic signet ring from the late seventh century BC was unearthed, inscribed in Hebrew with the name of a court official in Jeremiah's time.

Stone seal from the First Temple period discovered in Jerusalem in 2024.
(Israel National News, 2024. https://www.israelnationalnews.com/news/
395346)

These are only two examples. Such archaeological discoveries, though rare, nonetheless affirm the existence of events and people recorded in the Old Testament, and further validate the accuracy of the biblical record.

The Israelites were the People of the Book, so that was enough for them. Ironically, it is their Book that is still with us today, all over the world, while little else from that time survives.

JOSHUA

Joshua and Caleb were the **two spies** who said, "Let's go for it!" and were ignored by the obstinately fearful people of Israel. When the resistant generation had died during the wilderness wandering, the second-generation Israelites entered their Promised Land, forty years after leaving Egypt.

Trained by Moses, Joshua was now their leader. He had received the writing skills and a heart for God. Upon crossing the Jordan, Joshua diligently organized the people as Moses had. He also followed the presentation method used by Moses: reading the Law to the people as they stood to receive it (see Joshua 8).

A crowd that numbered almost two million people could not hear one speaker, in one reading. Did they rotate in groups of manageable size? Did Joshua delegate readers to different groups? The Children of Israel had twelve established tribal identities. A likely explanation is that tribal leaders would hear from Joshua, receive a copy, and then read from it to their clan leaders, who then received a copy to read to their clans.

Leaders reading the Torah in a city (De Luan/Alamy Stock Photo).

This tradition—**standing when the Scripture is read aloud**—continues to this day in many synagogues, and in churches as well. A copy of the Torah was also kept beside the Ark of the Covenant where it rested in the Tabernacle. For that relatively short period after the conquest, the Israelites led by Joshua honored the Scripture and God as they began to live in their new land.

COPYING AND SCRIBING

In Scripture, is there evidence of its own production by the people? Of equal importance is **its protection and presentation** to the people. Is any found in its own pages? Yes, and it is found in **the matrix of the Old Testament, a metaphorical weave of fabric** in which the whole is bound together. This fabric is the God-loving scribes, priests, elders, and prophets. Even some judges and kings joined many individual Israelites in prizing the Book of the Law.

The evidence does not scream. In some places the remnant of faithful Israelites is barely discernible, yet it is there. Elsewhere, a parade of evidence reveals the fabric loudly and outright, and all the more as the story of the Book progresses.

Can you imagine the original Torah written in Moses' hand? Yet over the years, even those five precious scrolls would deteriorate, becoming unusable and unreadable. Often, these aged scrolls were carefully placed in storage vessels named *gerizim* and buried.

All Torah scrolls would age from time and use, so the scribes, priests, Levites, and possibly tribal elders **carefully copied the scrolls and tended to their**

safety. It makes sense that this preservation activity became traditional for a People of the Book and is still used today.

NEGLECT

The Israelites had the benefit of a godly start to their national life in the Promised Land, thanks to Joshua and his generation. We see in the book of Joshua that the Law was read to the people and treasured in the land. But another generation arose, *who knew neither the Lord nor what he had done for Israel* (Judges 2:10).

Thus an attack on Scripture started in earnest: **neglect.** Everyone was doing what was right in his own eyes, ignoring what God's Law instructed (see Judges 21:25). The cycle of captivity by enemies, next followed by God's deliverance, prevailed for hundreds of years. During that time, little is mentioned of the Books of the Law, a glaring sign of neglect.

The Tabernacle was in Shiloh, where a copy of the Law would have been. The Ark of the Covenant and its copy of the Law was in Bethel, where some Israelites fasted, prayed, and sought advice from a godly priest with burnt offerings and fellowship offerings (see Judges 20:26–28). This reflects a shift to ritual-centered religion. As a dim remembrance, the Torah of Moses was neglected and pushed away by many Israelites. But always **a remnant of observant Israelites** lived and honored the Torah, people open to God who were taught by priests and Levites.

Yet the Torah remained still in the background, **woven into the fabric** of their identity. When two additional compositions were created—the books of Joshua and Judges—their authors spoke of the Law of God. This fact alone signifies that **a remnant community** within Israel studied, protected, and copied the Torah. As the future Bible waited to become front and center, it still shaped the lives of the loyal, who were not consumed by idolatry.

Those two books, Joshua and Judges, were soon joined with the Torah in the preservation efforts. Together, they survived neglect, and will again.

AUTHORSHIP

A word about authorship in Old Testament times: Our contemporary practices of authorship do not apply to ancient societies. Some books have identified authors, such as Moses' Torah, some of the Psalms, and the Prophets. Other books' authors are unknown, such as the books of history. Joshua probably authored the book bearing his name but we are not certain. It makes no such claim, and therefore may be written in his name; that's called an **eponymous writing**.

Not knowing a book's author does not make it less biblical, because authorship then was different from today. Our concepts of copyrights, libel, and even the plagiarism stigma were unknown when the Old Testament was created. Those legal realities were needed for our explosion of knowledge and technology, but for ancient society, writing was an act of *gravitas*. Whatever was written deserved the contribution of a wise posse to produce something lasting, transcendent to both individual tastes and transient time periods.

In addition, having an amanuensis or scribe write your book was a common practice in those times, and in no way diminished original authorship. Like today's authors collaborate with ghostwriters, the final work is released only upon the author's approval.

An ancient author in a desert tent dictating to a scribe. (Image generated by ChatGPT, OpenAI, 2025.)

For 1 and 2 Samuel, Esther, 1 and 2 Chronicles, and others, we perceive that the author had close knowledge of the events presented, that he could write or dictate, and that he was part of Israel's God-loving community. That's enough for us. People originally preserved these books, copied them, and included them as holy books, and why? Because in its own days, each book was known to be **a true account** of the times and the actions of God and people.

THE SPIRITUAL DESERT

After Judges, a period of prophets and kings arose. Read between the lines of the Samuels, the Chronicles, and the Kings. You'll see that the Torah and other collected books were well known to the priests in Shiloh, to Samuel and the other prophets, as well as to the priests and Levites during Israel's unity under Saul, David, and Solomon.

Yet there are no public readings recorded during that period, nor study of the Scripture by individuals. In its place is the sacrificial worship system. If someone wanted to consult the Torah, Writings or Prophets on any topic at all, great effort would be required. This spiritual desert is described: *In those days the word of the Lord was rare; there were not many visions* (1 Samuel 3:1).

In addition, the Ark of the Covenant was moved around with no mention of Scripture attending it. The Israelites converted the Ark of the Covenant into a weapon of war, and suffered for it. Their worship center in Shiloh was destroyed by the Philistines, who also suffered from their capture of the Ark (see 1 Samuel 6).

The people were mostly **dependent on meetings** where the Book of the Law was read to them, or so it appears. Maybe it was possible for them to seek out an individual to read it to them. Whatever the case, when the attack of **neglect** was abroad in the land, all Israelites suffered spiritually.

But in King David's reign, a dramatic spiritual improvement arose for Israel.

THE KINGS

Occasionally during the time of Samuel and the Kings, the whereabouts and use of the Scripture shines forth. Moses prophetically revealed instruction for Israel's future kings. Notice the implied responsibility of the priests and Levites to keep and preserve the scrolls of the Law:

> When [a king] takes the throne of his kingdom, he is to write for himself on a scroll a copy of this law, taken from that of the Levitical priests. It is to be with him, and he is to read it all the days of his life so that he may learn to revere the Lord his God and follow carefully all the words of the law and these decrees. (Deuteronomy 17:18–19, insert added)

Samuel saw the evil as well as good results of installing a kingship. Knowing the importance of a written constitution to regulate government, Samuel wrote important regulations.

> Samuel explained to the people the rights and duties of kingship. He wrote them down on a scroll and deposited it before the LORD. (1 Samuel 10:25)

Where would that document reside *before the* LORD? Shiloh had been destroyed; the Ark had become mobile; the Tabernacle was in Nob where the refugee David would take the consecrated bread for his soldiers (see 1 Samuel 21). Mizpah, where Samuel warned the people about a king, is a possible location which held repeated significance for early Israel. Perhaps Samuel placed it on a worship altar in his home in Ramah. The Scripture doesn't solve such curiosity of details, focusing instead upon **profound realities that transcend time** and place, and only the details needed for that focus.

If ever a king followed the prophetic instruction of Moses, it was **David**. Despite his descent into adultery and murder, he so sincerely repented. No other king of God's people left so powerful a testimony of love for the Lord and His Law. He wrote Psalm 119 and its 176 verses about the Law. Indeed, David's influence on Israel was the most widespread and deep, more than any other king or leader.

David dancing before the returning Ark. (Image generated by ChatGPT, OpenAI, 2025.)

In his most loyal advisors, we have a glimpse of Scripture's keepers—

Abiathar the priest, Nathan the prophet, and Zadok the priest. David's last words to Solomon affirm that the Scripture was close to him throughout his life and reign:

> So be strong, act like a man, and observe what the LORD your God requires: Walk in obedience to him, and keep his decrees and commands, his laws and regulations, as written in the Law of Moses. Do this so that you may prosper in all you do and wherever you go. (1 Kings 2:2–3)

Solomon did act that way, for a while. His dedication of the new Temple shows the common honor given to the Law of Moses. The community of official copyists and scribes is also assumed in his prayer:

> Praise be to the LORD, who has given rest to his people Israel just as he promised. Not one word has failed of all the good promises he gave through his servant Moses. May the LORD our God be with us as he was with our ancestors; may he never leave us nor forsake us. May he turn our hearts to him, to walk in obedience to him and keep the commands, decrees, and laws he gave our ancestors. And may these words of mine, which I have prayed before the LORD, be near to the LORD our God day and night, that he may uphold the cause of his servant and the cause of his people Israel according to each day's need, so that all the peoples of the earth may know that the LORD is God and that there is no other. And may your hearts be fully committed to the LORD our God, to live by his decrees and obey his commands, as at this time. (1 Kings 8:56–61)

During the reign of David, the spiritual desert was a thing of the past, at least temporarily. The Law of Moses became even more woven into the fabric of life for the People of the Book. Next to the Ark in the Tabernacle (and later the Temple), a copy of the Torah rested comfortably. Synagogues today honor that century-long tradition, preserving the Torah with ceremony in a special box, purposely named *Ark*.

DIVIDED KINGDOM

After Solomon, **the kingdom split in two, never to reunify**. In the biblical histories of the next four centuries, the northern kingdom is called Israel and the southernmost kingdom is called Judah. Despite their kinship, the two fought each other frequently.

The southern two tribes of Judah and Benjamin called Jerusalem their capital. The Temple worship and Davidic traditions kept them closer to the religion of Moses. The remaining ten tribes made Samaria their capital in the north.

Jerusalem and the Temple were not that far away from the northern kingdom. Israel's first king Jeroboam wanted to relieve his subjects from worshiping in a different kingdom, and established two alternative worship centers, Bethel and Luz. Thus Israel took the first steps to becoming the more corrupt of the two kingdoms. Because Jerusalem was the home to the Law of Moses (and the scribal community), Scripture eventually faded in significance for the northern kingdom.

In both these kingdoms remained many people who respected the Torah and other holy books. Some moved from Israel to Judah the southern kingdom, where Scripture was preserved and presented by the

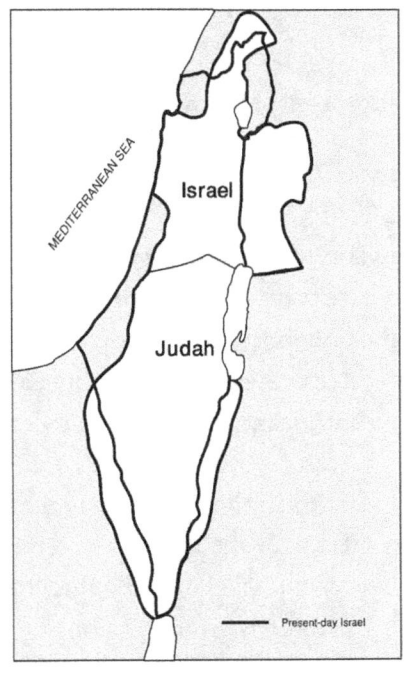

God's people split into two kingdoms: Israel in the north and Judah in the south. ("Ancient Jewish History: The Two Kingdoms." Jewish Virtual Library, 2025. https://www.jewishvirtuallibrary.org/the-two-kingdoms-of-israel)

priests and Levites. But in both kingdoms, many prophets risked their lives to rebuke the kings and people with warnings not to forsake the Law or worship idols.

And so it went, for several centuries. The families in the northern kingdom who loved the true God and His Law stayed as long as they could, yet the biblical histories reveal that many gradually migrated to the kingdom of Judah as Israel in the north became more Law-less.

The **thread of the prophets' activity is woven throughout** this period of the divided kingdoms. The Law is rarely mentioned, but the warnings of the prophets show they had studied it. We may rightly assume it was still kept by priests and Levites so this could occur.

In addition, the Lord's expectations were clear, as only the preserved Torah could convey. With a frequently repeated phrase, the preserved books reported that some kings "did what was right in the eyes of the LORD" (2 Chron. 25:2). Such kings would again clear the temple of idols, tear down Asherah poles, and restrict idol worship in the land.

BY A THREAD

Israel the northern kingdom was captured by Assyria and exiled in about 722 BC. The southern kingdom of Judah limped along for about one hundred twenty more years, with an occasional good king intermingled among evil ones. There were **always faithful elders, priests, and prophets in Judah** who kept the holy books and studied them.

Near the end of this time, an amazing event occurred under King Josiah after he authorized renewal construction on the Temple:

> Hilkiah the high priest said to Shaphan the secretary, "I have found the Book of the Law in the temple of the Lord." He gave it to Shaphan, who read it. . . . Then Shaphan the secretary informed the king, "Hilkiah the priest has given me a book." And Shaphan read from it in the presence of the king. (2 Kings 22:8, 10)

This book had been **neglected** by the kings and priests, even as it was protected in the Temple for such a moment as this. King Josiah's response was a righteous one: repentance and mourning (see 2 Kings 22:11). Upon hearing the consequences and warnings for disobedience to the Law of God, he could see Judah's fate looming in the future.

Second Kings 23 describes the sincerity of King Josiah's actions and the cooperation of his subjects. The fabric of Scripture, long **interwoven in their society**, was able to spring to life. Once again, it permeated the affairs of God's people. Josiah first called an assembly of all his subjects at the Temple, when, for the first time in centuries, they heard the Law read aloud—by the king, no less. As a part of the ceremony, the king and the people renewed the covenant with God as the Book instructed.

With their cooperation in the nationwide revival, Josiah next led Judah in a massive removal of idols in the land. Josiah oversaw a renewed celebration of the Passover as it was written in the Book of the Covenant. Finally, he rid the kingdom of all spiritualists, witches, and mediums.

MANY RIGHTEOUS

About two hundred years before King Josiah and his subjects in Judah received correction from the Law of Moses, the prophet Elijah triumphed over the prophets of the pagan god Baal, at Mt. Carmel. Yet the people did not receive the correction, and Elijah had a very human meltdown. God's response to him is revealing:

> Yet I reserve seven thousand in Israel—all whose knees have not bowed
> down to Baal and whose mouths have not kissed him. (1 Kings 19:18)

God's statement to Elijah and Josiah's revival give us a window into what was the case all along. **Not everyone forsook God** to take up idolatry. It is not a stretch to think this remnant had access to the Scripture. The Scriptures of the Lord remained vital in the hands of the godly.

MORE ADDED

For the production of Scripture, the times of kings in Israel and Judah were busy times. Their history was written and added to the cache of the Book: Judges, the Samuels, the Kings, and the Chronicles. The wisdom books were added as well: the Books of Psalms by David and others, as well as Solomon's Proverbs, Song, and Ecclesiastes.

Even during its neglect by the nation at large, the Scripture was preserved by the priests, Levites, prophets, elders, and occasional kings. Worn copies were reverently disposed of, and more copies produced by these quiet, meticulous heroes. This process also involved careful study of the Scripture as well, so that **the Book lived in the memory, minds, actions, and hearts of those who loved it.**

In its pages, you can hear David and Josiah, see Elijah, and relate to other notables the Scripture describes. But the identities of many others are not recorded. Together as a community within Israel, they did what God admonished Joshua when first entering the land:

> Be careful to obey all the law my servant Moses gave you; do not turn
> from it to the right or to the left, that you may be successful wherever
> you go. Keep this Book of the Law always on your lips; meditate on it day

and night, so that you may be careful to do everything written in it. (Joshua 1:7–8)

DURING THE EXILE

In 605 BC, the Babylonians began the first of three recorded deportations of Israelites from Judah. After these ravages, only a comparatively few poor were left; around them, Jerusalem and its Temple were demolished, their beautiful valuable implements all taken to Babylon.

But with the exiles went the Law of Moses and the other holy books. Without a Temple, the practice of meeting in **synagogues** became front and center, which continues to this day. There they worshiped God and were spiritually enriched by the Law. By this practice, the Jews maintained their identity and confirmed their repentance for idolatry.

Because of their origin in Judah and Jerusalem, the **Israelites came to be called Jews.** In Babylon and other places of exile, they were allowed to work, practice their religion, and prosper.

THE RETURN

The return of the Jews to Jerusalem happened as Jeremiah had prophesied: about seventy years after their exile. Rebuilding the Temple was the focus at first, followed later by the rebuilding of the city walls. With these objectives came the drama of foreign funding and intense local opposition.

As they had been deported in waves, likewise the return was in waves. We tend to think that all of the Jews in exile returned as quickly as they could to Jerusalem, but this was not the case. Only about 47,000 returned over the years in several waves. The other exiled Jews were scattered throughout the Middle East and its environs, including a large retinue in Egypt. Wherever they went, they established synagogues as best they could. Not all synagogues likely had a full Torah, but collected as many portions as they could, with Writings and Prophets that had been added.

The return of the Jews to Jerusalem had an additional characteristic. **Teaching the Law to the people enjoyed a large revival** under the leadership of Ezra—a scholar, scribe, and priest. Ezra had grown up during the exile. For him to know the Law as he did means that the holy books had gone with the Jews during the exile, and were available for study. About one hundred forty years after the last deportation in 585 BC, their renowned teacher and leader

Ezra taught the Book effectively from deep knowledge.

Ezra brought with him many faithful priests, Levites, heads of families, and others with a primary mission: to teach the Law to the people and exemplify obedience to the Law. This assembly of teachers held at least two public readings of the Law (see Nehemiah 8:3; 13:1). All the returnees stood for hours to hear it. In addition, teachers of the Law were placed in the crowd to explain the teaching.

Public reading of the Law was reinstated as a regular practice. The Book of Moses, which had been in the background of public life and survived the years of spiritual desert, now came to the forefront—setting a new tone for Jewish life in the Second Temple era.

Jews rebuilding the Temple after their return from Babylonian exile. (Image generated by ChatGPT, OpenAI, 2025.)

THE GATHERING OF THE BOOKS

Remember, the People of the Book did not call it "the Old Testament" at this time. Instead, the Book was known by its three types of content: the Torah, the Writings, and the Prophets.

In the background, outlasting the drama of the exile and return, the usual heroes—faithful priests, Levites, prophets, elders, and other Israelites—would husband these precious documents. Meticulously copying and teaching them, this corps would be petitioned by all the new synagogues for copies of the Law. The decree of Artaxerxes in Ezra 7 signifies that even the king himself received instruction in the Law:

> Whatever the God of heaven has prescribed, let it be done with diligence
> for the temple of the God of heaven. Why should his wrath fall on the
> realm of the king and of his sons? (Ezra 7:23)

For the previous centuries, Torah enjoyed a place of honor beside the Ark of the Covenant. When the Temple was rebuilt, the Torah and other holy books were restored to their place near the altar. In addition, the holy books were kept in an ark in the synagogue formed wherever a group of Jews had copies of them.

The care and reverence afforded these scrolls is hard to overstate. With no

Temple available outside of Jerusalem, the scattered population of Jews was called the **Diaspora**. The scrolls of Scripture were their lifeline to their God and worship.

COMPLETED CANON

By now, with the addition of the historical books, Ezra and Nehemiah, what we now call the canon of the Old Testament was very near completion. These holy books existed not only in Jerusalem but also in other Israelite settlements and synagogues throughout the known world.

Books of the Old Testament

BOOK	AUTHOR	DATE WRITTEN	TYPE OF WRITING
JOB	Unknown	Unknown	Poetry/Wisdom
GENESIS	Moses	1446–1406 BC	Narrative/Law
EXODUS	Moses	1446–1406 BC	Narrative/Law
LEVITICUS	Moses	1446–1406 BC	Narrative/Law
NUMBERS	Moses	1446–1406 BC	Narrative/Law
DEUTERONOMY	Moses	1446–1406 BC	Narrative/Law
JOSHUA	Unknown (possibly Joshua or Samuel)	1300s BC	Narrative
JUDGES	Unknown (possibly Samuel)	1350–1000 BC	Narrative
RUTH	Unknown (possibly Samuel)	1350–1000 BC	Narrative
1 AND 2 SAMUEL	Unknown	1100–931 BC	Narrative
PSALMS	David (73 psalms) Asaph (12 psalms) Sons of Korah (11 psalms) Other writers	1000–450 BC	Song/Poetry
PROVERBS	Solomon and others	900s–700s BC	Poetry/Wisdom
ECCLESIASTES	Unknown (possibly Solomon)	900s or 500s BC	Wisdom
SONG OF SONGS	Possibly Solomon and/or later writers	900s or 500s BC	Song/Poetry
JONAH	Jonah	783–753 BC	Narrative/Prophecy

BOOK	AUTHOR	DATE WRITTEN	TYPE OF WRITING
AMOS	Amos	760–753 BC	Prophecy
HOSEA	Hosea	752–722 BC	Prophecy
ISAIAH	Isaiah	740–681 BC	Prophecy
MICAH	Micah	738–698 BC	Prophecy
NAHUM	Nahum	663–612 BC	Prophecy
ZEPHANIAH	Zephaniah	641–628 BC	Prophecy
JEREMIAH	Jeremiah	626–582 BC	Prophecy
HABAKKUK	Habakkuk	609–598 BC	Prophecy
DANIEL	Daniel	605–535 BC	Narrative/Prophecy
EZEKIEL	Ezekiel	593–571 BC	Prophecy
LAMENTATIONS	Jeremiah	586 BC	Lament
OBADIAH	Obadiah	586 BC	Prophecy
1 AND 2 KINGS	Unknown	561–539 BC	Narrative
HAGGAI	Haggai	520 BC	Prophecy
ZECHARIAH	Zechariah	520–518 BC	Prophecy
1 AND 2 CHRONICLES	Unknown (possibly Ezra)	450–400 BC	Narrative
EZRA	Ezra	400s BC	Narrative
NEHEMIAH	Ezra	400s BC	Narrative
ESTHER	Unknown	400s BC	Narrative
MALACHI	Malachi	400s BC	Prophecy
JOEL	Joel	Unknown (possibly 400s BC)	Prophecy

All dates are approximate. Books are listed in the order in which they're believed to have been written, not the order they appear within the biblical narrative.

Charts from *How We Got the Bible Made Easy* ©2020. Used by permission of Rose Publishing/Tyndale House. All rights reserved.

A MESS—A HOT MESS!

During the century after the Return, the 47,000 returnees rebuilt Jerusalem, with its wall and its Temple. The spiritual desert of the past was replaced with spiritual revival. The teaching of Ezra and his cohorts brought a renewal of respect for the Torah.

The land of the Jews next entered **a time of turmoil** beginning about 400 BC. These four centuries came to be called the silent years because there was no prophet, whether of the stature of Isaiah or any writing prophet. The Jews concluded God remained silent. Nothing was added to the Old Testament; the New Testament was not composed until after Jesus' time. Therefore these four hundred years are called the inter-testamental period. (Another name for this time is the Second Temple period.)

Frequently, when I think about tough times in history, I wonder, "Where would be the best place to ride out these difficult years—or maybe even prosper? What work would provide both a living and a measure of safety?" I was hard-pressed to identify any place or work during those inter-testamental years that offered safety, for there was precious little.

Why so difficult? Why call it a hot mess?

In brief, the Jews were challenged at all times on all sides. Rarely independent, Judea was intermittently oppressed by the Persians, the Greeks, the Seleucids, the Hasmoneans, and finally the Romans. In addition, internal wars, strife, and oppression make even their survival seem miraculous.

HAMMER ON JEWISH LIFE

Jewish religious life became fractured under this cultural pressure. The diverse responses among Jews led to a seemingly never-ending strife, both internal and external. Imagine **a giant hammer hit Jewish life**, and especially their religious life, sending its pieces scattered all over Judea.

One piece became Hellenized. Another piece became the cult of the Temple—Pharisees, Sadducees, and Scribes (who had become teachers more than copyists). Highly religious, highly political, and wealthy, their center of influence was Jerusalem.

Other groups became hyper-religious and withdrew to the desert areas. The Essenes in Qumran were one such—a monastic community in the wilderness. Yet another example are the radicals who called themselves Sicari or Zealots. They performed acts of rebellion or assassination as their Jewish duty.

But what about **the many observant Jews** in the Diaspora, living outside Jerusalem? This group, the largest, depended on their synagogues for spiritual and biblical instruction. It was also a center of social life and hospitality. The greatest population of the Jews was simply trying to make do with what was available.

A hot mess: Jewish society under the hammer. (Image generated by ChatGPT, OpenAI, 2025.)

Notably, the disciples and followers of Jesus reflected all these diverse groups. Jesus chose the Sicari Zealot, Simon, and in contrast, Matthew (Levi) was a Jewish tax collector for the Romans. Andrew and John were disciples of John the Baptist whose lifestyle mirrored that of the Qumran Essenes, while Simon and James learned their faith from synagogue rulers like Jairus. And after the Holy Spirit was poured out, many of the Levitical priests put their faith in Jesus. Apostle Paul had been a strict Pharisee, as was Nicodemus. Even the Roman Cornelius was included.

HELLENIZATION

Perhaps even more insidious than direct military attack, a cultural challenge raged in Judea: Hellenization, meaning pressure to act Greek. This pressure first arose under Alexander of Macedonia, whose lieutenants and governors imposed the requirements of Greek culture upon conquered peoples. The subsequent Roman occupiers heavily encouraged the resulting cultural norms.

The Greeks had a unique approach to conquering other nations. Instead of taking slaves or deporting the conquered population, they built Greek cities in the newly conquered territory. But the ideal Jewish lifestyle and ideal Greek behavior were antithetical in almost every way. Therefore, the Jews faced many pressures, especially economic pressures, to conform to Greek life—both in Judea and in their worldwide dispersion.

In order to do business or prosper, the **Jews were challenged to participate in pagan rituals** or at least give alms to the Greek gods at yearly festivals. Nudity in public was shameful for Jewish men, yet that was expected in the baths, gymnasia, and footraces of the Greeks. To be an observant Jew meant refraining from such activities, and refraining was costly financially, socially, and politically. The Jews who conformed to Greek life to any extent were accused of being Hellenized, and were scorned by more observant Jews. This created a rift among Jews which sometimes came to blows. Reaction to Hellenization fractured their unity, family, and their adherence to the Laws of God and their Scripture.

SCRIPTURES PRESERVED

During all this mess, the Torah and other holy books were still being preserved and copied. They were used in the Temple and in synagogues throughout Judea and the Empire's Jewish communities, the Diaspora. The long-standing habit of treasuring the Scripture continued as the habit of the Jews. Still in scroll form, they were also known and preserved throughout the Diaspora.

So, it is still hard to see how these books could have been heavily edited (*redacted*) during these years. Observant Jews would have seen through such an effort, and forbidden it. Such a monumental change in the holy books could not escape notice. Instead, a tsunami of outcry and protest would have resulted and left historical evidence plain to all.

Outside Judea, who could have made the effort to obtain and edit ALL existing Torahs and holy books? No record exists of such an effort. It seems that two or more Torahs would have emerged—edited ones and unedited ones. There is **not a hint of evidence** for this.

FIRST TRANSLATION

A major first occurred during these years of national turmoil and prophetic silence. The Jewish holy books were **translated into another language**. For the first time, non-Hebrew speakers had access to read the Scripture in Greek.

This significant translation came out of Alexandria, a center of scholarship in the Egyptian delta. Its magnificent and famous library held readable copies of most of the books available in the known world. Koine Greek was *lingua franca*, the language of all the cultural and economic world. People spoke and wrote it all over the Roman Empire, making it a universal language at the time.

Meanwhile, Hebrew became less understood by the majority of Jews, especially among the Diaspora. Hebrew speakers were distinguished with the phrase, "Hebrew of Hebrews," as Apostle Paul described himself three hundred years later. Thus a Greek translation of the Torah, and later the Writings and the Prophets, was sorely needed. Called the Septuagint, it was a Greek translation of what we now call the Old Testament.

We know that the translation from Hebrew to Greek occurred in about 250 BC. Its name, *Septuagint*, comes from the history that seventy scholars produced it, although legends surround its production. Abbreviated using the Roman numerals for seventy, LXX, the Septuagint is still usable today for matters of biblical scholarship. It is also used currently in the Greek Orthodox Church.

BIBLE-BURNING

An offensive attack was made on the scrolls of the Jews' Bible during these intertestamental years. Antiochus IV, so-called Epiphanes, was a Seleucid ruler of Judea responsible for the desecration of the Temple in Jerusalem in about 168 BC. He set up a pagan idol inside it and oversaw **a pig sacrifice on its altar**. When Antiochus ordered the Temple's Scripture scrolls burned, he entered the record as the first ruler outside Judaism who recognized that they were a People of the Book, and thus tried to destroy the Bible.

As an effort to exterminate Scripture, it was futile—as it is now. But his effort revealed the depth to which the holy books were woven into Jewish life.

The actions of Antiochus Epiphanes IV caused an uproar that lasted many years and inspired an armed response from the Jews—the Maccabean Revolt.

THE BIRTH AND LIFE OF JESUS

Where in this hot mess did God plan to send the beloved Son who had been prophesied? As it turned out, Jesus was born to an observant family of Jews in the Galilee. In Jesus' lifetime, this area had many advantages. Among them was enough food and necessities for life, for this was not a time of drought or hunger. Because of the *Pax Romana,* the danger of major attacks by foreign armies, customary in previous centuries, was remote.

Due to past translations of the Gospels' Greek word *tekton*, Jesus is often called a carpenter. But as we use the word today, our English meaning for "carpenter" is too narrow. In today's English, a better word would be subcontractor or builder.

Nazareth was near Sepphoris, a Greek city being rebuilt during Jesus' lifetime. As an easy walk from Nazareth, Sepphoris provided work for a *tekton*—a builder—which was Jesus' profession and that of His family. Much of the gospel record is explained by this, such as His knowledge of the Greek and Roman languages, His understanding of their cultures, and some imagery in His parables.

Underground reservoir at Sepphoris (image by J. Robert Teringo). (Richard A. Batey. *Jesus & the Forgotten City: New Light on Sepphoris and the Urban World of Jesus.* Baker Publishing Group, 1992.)

The synagogue in Nazareth provided the town's spiritual life, possibly directed by local teachers and visiting rabbis. Thus the young Jesus could be **hands on and face to face with Scripture**, in ways that wouldn't have been easy if He had grown up in Jerusalem. Being distant from the Temple, which He visited for feasts, protected Him from the taint of the politicized leaders there until His ministry began.

We know through the New Testament record that Jesus was well-versed in the Torah, the Writings, and the Prophets. Never being formally trained in Jerusalem, as were the Scribes and Pharisees, it was to His advantage because He

37

avoided the corruption they exhibited. Familiar with their debate habits, He could stand up to any argument or puzzle they presented. He did this with common rabbinic methods such as posing questions and stating the obvious. By using the Jewish Scripture handily, Jesus could get to the heart of the matter. He was called *Rabbi*—Teacher—in the Gospels, because like all rabbis, He was systematically trained in the synagogue from a young age and traveled with disciples.

Jesus' ministry showed His care to adhere to the pattern of a rabbi of that day: Memorize most of the Scripture, learn to read and write Hebrew, learn to present dialectical arguments (as seen in the movie *Yentl*), and have disciples. This was not formal training as we think of it, but it was His best path to the most vigorous spiritual life. After all, the Jewish religion of that day was shattered into pieces, and **He successfully avoided the extremes** of the Essenes, the Zealots, and the Temple cult.

So, this was the world in which the followers of Jesus were raised. In those days the Scripture was in the Temple, in synagogues all over Judea, and in the scattered communities of the Jewish Diaspora throughout the Roman Empire. In eastern and western settlements alike, down into Egypt—everywhere in the known world—the writings of the Jews were available.

While a few could read the holy books for themselves, mostly they listened to them at least weekly in the synagogues. There, a portion of the Torah was read along with portions from both the Writings and the Prophets. If the listeners were limited to the Aramaic language, someone would translate for them.

The Scripture, as well as the traditions built up around it, were **faithfully copied** and reverently disposed of when outworn from use. Scrolls were the universal form, both on papyrus and occasionally on treated animal skins known as parchment. The scrolls were stored in boxes mostly, and fiercely protected by the Jews—holy books not only on scrolls but **also in their hearts through life and practice for about 1,400 years.**

CHAPTER 3

___

THE NEW CHURCH TO MARTIN LUTHER

A WORLD OF CHANGE: AD 33 TO 1517

WHAT A CRAZY, HEADY TIME THAT MUST HAVE BEEN FOR THE disciples, the other followers of Jesus, and indeed all of Jerusalem! With the death of Jesus sending everyone involved into the depths of despair, then into the heights of joy with His resurrection—it was an emotional mess! Being with Jesus and seeing Him taken into heaven just added to the drama!

But that's not all. The original disciples and others waited in the Upper Room for—well, they didn't know, not until the Holy Spirit fell on them in a most dramatic way, with the sound of a mighty wind and tongues of fire. This was **a first in human history**—the Holy Spirit of God poured out on anyone following Jesus. After this, **thousands were added to their number.** (I bet there were!) Many foreigners were in the city for the Pentecost feast, and later traveled home with the gospel. The Church of Jesus was born.

What to do with all of this going forward?

BELIEVERS SEARCH SCRIPTURE

As things began to settle somewhat, a new group began to form: an *ekklesia*, Greek for a council gathering, which we now call the church. Meeting in synagogues, homes, and anywhere possible, the believers sang a new song of praise, read their Jewish Scripture with new eyes, and prayed. The teachings of Jesus, **both remembered and written**, were becoming a new part of the traditional teaching.

Searching the Scriptures went on apace. Jews who became believers used their knowledge of the Torah, the Writings, and the Prophets, searching them for prophecies of Jesus. They found a treasure trove. He had been there in the Jewish Scriptures all along, and **they missed Him in its pages**. Only after He opened their minds (see Luke 24:45) did they see Him in it. Peter used their new insight when he cited Psalm 69:25 and 109:8 to explain Judas' betrayal of Jesus (see Acts 1).

Jesus' everyday, miraculous life and teachings were rapidly transmitted, both **in writing and in speech**. Now the written and oral treasures informed the teaching about Christ. A new and clearer picture has emerged from current research—yes, **many kept notes in writing**. Added to the oral skills of others, the new church maintained accurate memories of the Savior.

So the New Testament began. From these small beginnings, the first century Scriptures were forming.

THE CHURCH COMPILES THE NEW TESTAMENT

In recent centuries, prevailing opinion held that the Gospels were not written at all until the late 40s AD, with the rest of the New Testament even later. But it defies credulity to think that none of Jesus' earth-shaking life and teaching was written as people heard it, because the use of writing and literary skill was so prevalent.

It is likely that **many writings existed which were not saved for posterity or used formally.** Hence in the 40s and 50s AD, a movement in the church **formalized** the many written notes in good Koine Greek and on well-made parchment and papyrus. Thus was produced what became the New Testament, soon becoming holy to the new church.

Parchment was made of animal skins which were dried and stretched, and it became popular just in time for the compilation of the New Testament. Parchment added to the use of papyrus as the material of choice for writing, simultaneous with another useful technology for these new Scriptures: the **codex**.

For centuries, written sheets rolled into scrolls had prevailed as the format for all written material. But when sheets were folded in quarters or eights, called a quire, pages were formed. Quires then stitched down the middle formed the codex, which was far more useful and versatile. Joined to other such folded sheets and sewn together, the quires became the very familiar book form used today.

One sheet folds twice to make a quire of eight pages. (Image from
University of Michigan Papyrology Collection.)

Christians really took advantage of this technology: small, perfectly portable, easy to read in church, and even easy to hide during persecutions. Carried abroad, codices (the plural of codex) enriched churches empire-wide.

While the *Pax Romana* (Latin for "peace of Rome") lasted, travel and trade routes were kept safe. Despite persecution and other obstacles, churches were spreading and prospering all over the Roman Empire—and with them, their Scriptures. The four Gospels of Matthew, Mark, Luke, and John had become the **cornerstones of the church**. Later the Epistles of Paul and letters of other apostles were added to the number.

*Codex Sassoon, a manuscript of the Jewish Bible in Hebrew (Camillo
Barone, Forward.com)*

At first, not all the new churches possessed copies of the above. One may have one or more of the Gospels. Another may have a collection of Paul's letters, or one or two. Churches shared among themselves; see Colossians 4:16 for an example of the practice. As time went on and copies multiplied, the books became a recognized collection, which is now our New Testament.

FALSITY THREATENS

But this was messy business. Many others wanted to write holy works. So, the field became very crowded with other so-called gospels and epistles. What to do to keep out **false works**?

The rise and eventual prevalence of heresies and false beliefs—especially about the person and work of Christ—forced the churches to decide which writings were legitimate and inspired. By the time these challenges become pressing, the churches had bishops and others to oversee the process.

The legitimacy was largely validated organically in local churches. Over multiple generations of Christians, it was well known **which writings passed the two tests**: written by original apostles (or a disciple of one), and read publicly in multiple churches with consistent spiritual effect. Which books were from the Holy Spirit was a less tangible test but was known by the Christians with practiced spiritual perception. Yet, even to this day, those false writings still haunt and allure, as chapter five will show.

SCRIPTURE TAKES SHAPE

Athanasius, Bishop of Alexandria, distributed a yearly address to all the churches. In AD 367, his address regarded the date of Easter (a big deal in those days). Almost like a postscript or afterthought at the end of the letter, he included a list of **acceptable books used in the churches**. Thus casually, Bishop Athanasius introduced the world to the canon of Scripture, which a church council formalized a few years later.

The bishop's list contained all of our current New Testament books. **The order of the books continued to differ** among versions, but the canonical books remain the same to this day.

BOOK	AUTHOR	DATE WRITTEN	TYPE OF WRITING
PHILEMON	Paul	AD 60–62	Letter to Philemon, a member of the church in Colossae
1 TIMOTHY	Paul	AD 62–66	Letter to Timothy, a pastor in Ephesus
1 PETER	Peter	AD 64	Letter to Christians in Asia Minor
2 PETER	Peter	AD 64	Letter to Christians in Asia Minor
TITUS	Paul	AD 64–66	Letter to Titus, a pastor in Crete
2 TIMOTHY	Paul	AD 66–67	Letter to Timothy, a pastor in Ephesus
HEBREWS	Unknown	AD 60s	Letter to Jewish Christians
JUDE	Jude	AD 60s–80s	Letter to Christians everywhere
JOHN	John	AD 85–95	Account (gospel) of the life of Jesus
1 JOHN	John	AD 85–95	Letter to Christians in Asia Minor
2 JOHN	John	AD 85–95	Letter to the "Elect Lady," which could mean the church
3 JOHN	John	AD 85–95	Letter to Gaius, a Christian in Asia Minor
REVELATION	John	AD 95	Apocalypse and letters churches in Asia Minor

BOOK	AUTHOR	DATE WRITTEN	TYPE OF WRITING
JAMES	James	AD 49	Letter to Jewish Christians across the Roman Empire
GALATIANS	Paul	AD 49	Letter to Christians in the region of Galatia
MARK	John Mark	AD 50s	Account (gospel) of the life of Jesus
1 THESSALONIANS	Paul	AD 50–51	Letter to Christians in Thessalonica
2 THESSALONIANS	Paul	AD 50–51	Letter to Christians in Thessalonica
1 CORINTHIANS	Paul	AD 55–56	Letter to Christians in Corinth
2 CORINTHIANS	Paul	AD 56	Letter to Christians in Corinth
ROMANS	Paul	AD 57	Letter to Christians in Rome
MATTHEW	Matthew (Levi)	AD 60s	Account (gospel) of the life of Jesus
LUKE	Luke	AD 60–62	Account (gospel) of the life of Jesus
ACTS	Luke	AD 60–62	History of the early church
EPHESIANS	Paul	AD 60–62	Letter to Christians in Ephesus
PHILIPPIANS	Paul	AD 60–62	Letter to Christians in Philippi
COLOSSIANS	Paul	AD 60–62	Letter to Christians in Colossae

Books are listed in the order in which they're believed to have been written. Dates are approximate and give a time span within which the book was written.

SORTING BY EARLY CHURCHES

People began writing what they considered to be holy books. The churches across the known world favored a variety of these writings which were not on Athanasius' list.

Some remain included in a section now know as the Apocrypha. The Apocryphal books were designated as beneficial and edifying, but not Scripture. They were included in many editions of the Bible and still remain respected in the Catholic Bible.

Other writings were disdained as false and spurious, and are often called the Pseudepigrapha. This Greek word designates them as books falsely claiming apostolic origin. One example is the so-called Gospel of Thomas which we will see in a coming chapter.

AS ROME DECLINES

Lastly, significant events affecting Scripture occurred in the last five hundred years of the Roman Empire, notably the following.

In about AD 120, the newly recognized canon of Scripture began to be called the **New Testament**—first by emerging Bible scholars, then the churches at large. The rise of such a name affected not only the new Scripture, but the long-established Scriptures. The Torah, the Writings, and the Prophets began to be called the **Old Testament**. These two new designations remain the same to this day.

The church was severely persecuted, first locally and sporadically, then later empire-wide. Yet the church of Jesus continued to spread and prosper. Their many cries to God produced an answer in an unlikely form: the Roman emperor Constantine. He declared the Church of Jesus legal in AD 313, thus ending the persecution. Later the church was declared **the official religion of the empire**.

Emperor Constantine ordered fifty Bibles to be produced and placed in the churches—created from the finest vellum, and copied by the best scribes. Two of the three best ancient examples of Bibles from this period—the Codices Vaticanus and Sinaiticus—may have been part of Constantine's order, although this can't be verified. Written in the finest scribal hand, these codices are used today in research to identify the best Greek text of the Scripture.

We should pause here to reflect. The Bible has always been cherished, faithfully copied, protected, memorized, and obeyed by the faithful, both publicly and privately. So much so, in fact, that it was impossible to be destroyed or changed in any significant ways. Does this look like God built in those safeguards? And no doubt, He used supernatural protections as required to keep His Word safe through the ages.

Bible scholars became authoritative interpreters of the Bible during the period **before the fall of the Roman Empire**. The most significant was St. Jerome, widely respected for his skill in Greek and Latin. He even studied Hebrew to get his translation just right. In his later years, about AD 400, he posted himself up in Bethlehem and compiled the Latin translation from the original Scripture languages. It became known as the Vulgate, still in use today.

THE BIBLE & THE FALL OF ROME

After the fall of the Roman Empire in the fourth and fifth centuries, the world of the Romans in general and the church specifically was shaken to its core. People everywhere sought to earn a living in safety, but there was little to find. Hordes of northern and eastern tribesmen pressed in as Rome's protective umbrella crashed, and the darkness of this age fell upon the next five centuries.

As the literacy rate plummeted, materials for book production which were previously cheap and abundant became scarce and very expensive. Now the time is called the Early Middle Ages, but historians originally named it the Dark Ages, for indeed it was in many ways—especially economically and educationally.

Ethnic groups and their territories developed new governmental leadership, the seeds of today's countries, and actually got along, even helping each other for a while. Wherever the church at Rome held sway, its bishops and priests maintained its influence.

One way Christians sought safety was to build monasteries of all kinds. Some of these became centers of learning, while others became refuges and sanctuaries for the surrounding countryside. So, despite the social upheavals after empire collapse, Christians held on to their faith, and the church actually grew during this chaotic time.

The Bible remained in large book form, while becoming more and more alien to people outside church leadership. In Jerome's Latin translation, fewer people could read it as Latin faded from everyday usage with the fall of the Roman Empire. Bibles were **copied in monasteries and a few scriptoriums**, yet its cost soared as parchment became scarcer and thus very expensive.

The western churches of the Empire were governed by the bishop in Rome, who came to be known as the pope. The only people who had ready access to Scripture were monks and churchmen, and a few wealthy or politically connected individuals who could hire readers or become literate themselves.

CHARLEMAGNE

Famously crowned by surprise as Holy Roman Emperor in Rome on Christmas Day AD 800, the Frankish king Charles I ruled over the territory of modern France and regions beyond. Charles was considered a light in the darkness. It was not his way of ruling, his laws, nor his kingdom, but his effect on culture, learning, and especially the Bible. For this and other reasons he came to be called Charles the Great, a.k.a. Charlemagne.

He loved learning. Gathering manuscripts both secular and religious, he called the highly skilled from other parts of the empire to study in his new institutions of learning. One called from England was the renowned Bible scholar Alcuin. Not only scholars but others in book production were summoned, such as **illuminators**, artists who could adorn each page of the Bible with vivid colors and beautiful artistry.

An illuminated page from the Book of Kells, displayed at Trinity College in Dublin, Ireland. (Anne-Marie Diffley. "Why Is the Book of Kells Different?" Trinity College Dublin, 2024. https://www.visittrinity.ie/blog/why-is-the-book-of-kells-important/)

In this environment, many beautiful, illuminated editions of the Vulgate Bible (Jerome's Latin translation) were produced, which then set the standard for copyists for several hundred years. Larger numbers of the Bible were produced than ever before, thanks to Charlemagne's support for the Bible production industry.

Up to the time of Charlemagne, manuscripts known as *uncials* had been copied using a script called *majuscule;* we might call it uppercase letters. But during his reign, a new hand script was developed, much like our cursive, called *miniscule.* This sped and simplified the copying process, enabling more Bible production in the scriptoriums and monasteries.

THE MEDIEVAL BIBLE

Now moving to the Middle Ages (approximately AD 1000–1500), how were the **largely illiterate people in Christendom** supposed to survive spiritually? One way: Rome encouraged church and local authorities in every part to build churches and cathedrals—some elaborate, some not. We can see how the Roman church meant well at first, to help the illiterate by portraying Bible events. Over time, that purpose became subordinate to greed and abuse by both church and feudal leaders.

These places of worship were adorned with painted pictures of Jesus, a myriad of statues of saints, crucifixes, and the like. Larger establishments added beautiful stained-glass windows depicting biblical moments and persons—Adam and Eve, Abraham and Isaac, Moses, Elijah, many recognized church saints, and more. When building skills developed, cathedrals presented the people with soaring ceilings meant to lift the congregation's spirits to heaven. Add some incense and chants (such as Gregorian chants) and that was mostly it for lay people.

Over time, the church developed dramatic plays, first depicting Christmas and Easter. Churchmen served as actors in these plays. First set at the altar of the church, they came to be performed in the streets as well. The plays also began using real actors and regular citizens. The dramas then came to be performed on carts in towns across Europe.

THE BIBLE WITHHELD

Another transformation over time: Practically every day became a saint day. Proper veneration of each day's saint thus demanded increasing time and money from the congregation.

The leadership of many churches, from the neighborhood priest to the pope in Rome, developed a greedy and abusive stance toward their flock. Even the well-meaning among them thought it best to leave Christians at large ignorant of the whole Bible.

Anyone taught to read Scripture could compare the church they knew to the church of Scripture. The ignorance of the populace was protection against a threatening scrutiny for those church leaders, yet what they feared was soon to burst forth.

Here is how Dr. Bill Hamon expresses the situation in his 2011 book, *Prophetic Scriptures Yet to Be Fulfilled*:

> For more than a thousand years during the Dark Age, God's Church had been in bondage to a totalitarian religious system. Church members were slaves to religious ritual and to dead doctrines such as buying relics and

doing penance. There were no Bibles available for the people, so they had no way of knowing if what the Church hierarchy was dictating to them was according to the truth of God's Word. They were at the mercy of the clergy just as Israel was at the mercy of the slave masters. The Church members were whipped by the lashes of asceticism, thrown into solitary confinement by monasticism, and terrorized by the fires of purgatory, living in constant fear of eternal judgment by a wrathful God. The Church system that arose in the Dark Age claimed to have power to open and shut the doors of Heaven to any human being. There was more condemnation, paganism, and superstition than there was grace, pardon, and peace. (pp. 84–85)

A WARNING TO US ALL

Lest we see the Roman Catholic Church as the only corrupted body, any church, family, or individual can follow that path. It takes sacrificial vigilance, prayer, and righteous habits to prevent it. Even though the problems of medieval Catholicism may be evident, humility recognizes it isn't the only body to go astray over the centuries. We still see such corruption on a smaller scale today.

SUPERSTITION ARISES

Living on spiritual scraps, which the Roman Catholic Church in those days gave out sparingly, the people of Christendom developed many superstitious responses to difficult events. Author Hilary Mantel expressed this well in *The Mirror & the Light,* the third of her period trilogy:

> The common folk of England live on song and tales and alehouse jokes. Spending their pence on candles to burn before holy images, they live in the dark, and in the dark take fright. Let us say a calf is born dead. By the time the tale crosses a field, it is a calf with two heads. Cross a stream, and it is a calf with two heads, chanting backwards in Latin, and some friar is charging a shilling for a charm against it. So it goes, in half a day, from abortion to Antichrist; and somehow, everybody is poorer except the priests. Pastors warn their flocks that if they do not send tribute to Rome, trees will walk and crops will blight. They make them dread the fire of purgatory, which eats to the bones; they ask, can you bear to see

your dead folk burning—your helpless old mother, your dead little children, bound in agony and screaming for your prayers?

Now it is hard for them to hear the gospel news; there is no purgatory, only judgement. God is not a market trader, selling mercy by the pound. You cannot buy salvation, nor can you delegate a monk to work out your salvation for you. (p. 275)

Some **beliefs and behaviors became so extreme** as to stretch the limits of credulity. For example, Pope Gregory IX issued a papal bull against cats as demons, ordering them all killed. A massive and cruel extermination ensued. Ironically, these cats could have killed the rats that would bring the plague, or at least limit its spread.

The second of Mantel's trilogy, *Bring Up The Bodies,* puts it this way:

According to the custodians of holy relics, part of the power of these artefacts is that they are able to multiply. Bone, wood and stone have, like animals, the ability to breed, yet keep their intact nature; the offspring are in no wise inferior to the originals. So the crown of thorns blossoms. The cross of Christ puts out buds; it flourishes, like a living tree. Christ's seamless coat weaves copies of itself. Nails give birth to nails. (p. 69)

Well, the church folk had to explain the presence of one hundred toe bones from Saint Peter somehow!

STAND-INS PERMITTED

One ray of spiritual sunshine became widespread: **the Book of Hours**, sometimes contracted to Hours. This small book was so prevalent that many copies survive today; it was so popular that the first book printed in Arabic was a Book of Hours.

Book of Hours, ca. 1325 of Jeanne d'Evreux, Queen of France. (The Cloisters Collection, 1954, Object No. 54.1.2.)

Many copies were written on the finest vellum and illuminated by the best artists. Some were even mentioned in wills as a prized inheritance. But other, less ornate Hours became available to everyone as time passed. A kind of middle merchant class arose which could afford the less fancy copies. Such a copy of Hours was preserved for centuries in an Irish bog, and is now displayed in Ireland's Museum of Natural History.

But what was it about this Book of Hours? It was important not to arouse hostility from the pope or other prelates in church leadership, so this book had the church's eight canonical hours of prayer, with a perpetual calendar of Saint Days and illustrations like those in churches.

The sunshine was some important Scripture included in each Book of Hours. Many psalms graced their pages along with some of the Gospels and other Scripture. This was a step forward, simultaneous with the growth of a literate middle class. Local priests could translate the Scripture portions into the local language. Regular Christians could now read portions of the Scripture, a rapidly growing desire which facilitated the coming Reformation in the sixteenth century.

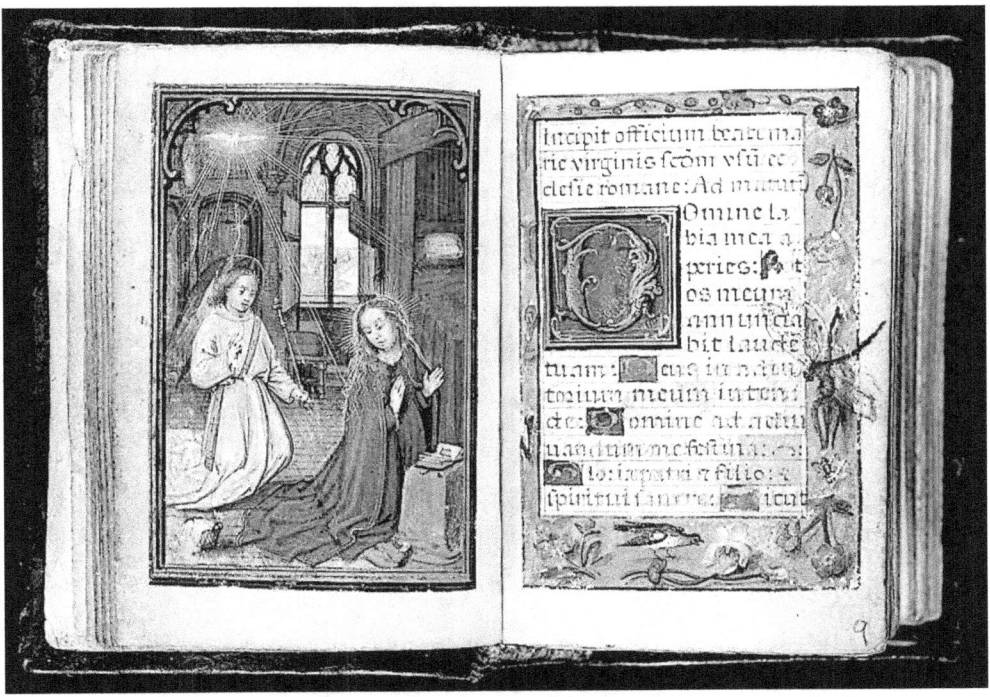

Book of Hours, ca. 1530 of Simon Bening. (The Cloisters Collection, 2015; Object No. 2015.706.)

THE FRIARS

Around the thirteenth century, a new order of clerics arose, called friars. When they were good, they were of great help to the people, but if not, they were corrupt like everyone else.

The ones who kept to their calling preached the gospel in the people's language. Sacrificially they helped the sick, fed the poor, and fought for what was right. In their pockets, they carried a tiny Bible, ready to minister. They knew Latin and could translate it into the vernacular. Although their ministry by nature produced few records, it's easy to imagine how many people were blessed by their biblical life.

THE BLACK DEATH

Rightly so was the Plague known as the Black Death, and later, the Great Mortality. The disease still occurs; its formal name now is *yersinia pestis*. If diagnosed in time, it can be cured with a simple antibiotic, but in the mid-fourteenth century, the sequence was much more dreadful. In AD 1349, the first wave of this wicked disease arrived from Western Asia via shipping lanes and caravan routes. We know now that the vectors (that is, carriers) were mostly fleas on certain species of rats. An infectious disease, it was also spread person to person via coughs, clothes, and touch.

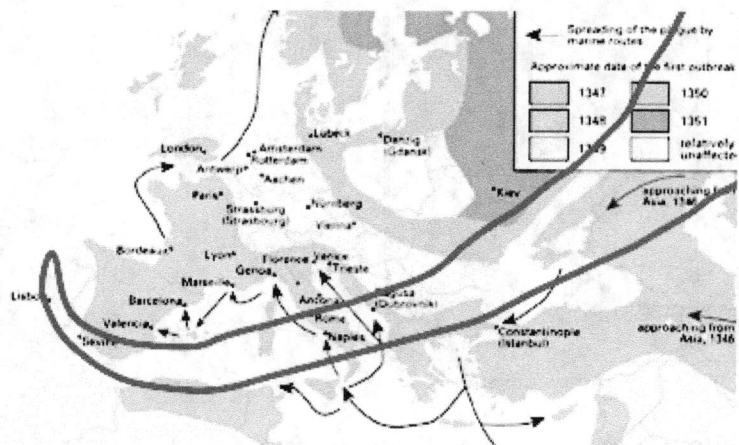

Sickle-shaped waves of the Black Death plague, ca. 1350.

In the shape of a huge sickle on the map of the Mediterranean Sea and Europe, the Black Death cut a swath from Western Asia, across the sea, then up through Western Europe, and then down through Eastern Europe. To these millions of people, it seemed to come on the wind or from the ground. We can only imagine what the superstitious minds of the Middle Ages believed.

The Great Mortality—what a time! A third to a half of the population died an agonizing death after being infected. The pneumonic form of the plague was 99.9 percent fatal; the systemic variant offered only the smallest hope of recovery.

For a long period, the Black Death resurfaced roughly every decade, although its virulence and fatality waned somewhat. Europe's population was severely reduced in number; culture became death-obsessed. Many decades passed before any rebound of normalcy from the cycles of this dreadful disease.

The Bible was indirectly affected by the Plague in an unexpected way. The Roman Church had so greatly dominated the minds and lives of Europe's population; yet in this great crisis, the church was mostly useless and powerless against it. To salvage some semblance of spiritual power, the Roman authorities resorted to unusual means. Yet, with very few exceptions, no candles, no prayer, no church ritual, nor sacrament could stop the Black Death. Not even the pope's so-called Babylonian exile in Avignon was spared—a fourth of his retinue perished during the papacy of Clement VI.

Aggravating the situation, many of the clergy abandoned their parishes, fleeing to the country and other locations they thought to be safer for them. These clergy did not even offer the last rites sacrament to those dying of the plague, and officiated no funeral services. Mass graves proliferated—the final shame of a horrible death. **People felt abandoned by their church**.

These forces combined to discredit the Roman Church leadership and to create more hunger among the people for a new and living way. More seeds of the Reformation were sown, with four rapid events to enable its cornerstone: the printed Bible!

AS THE AGE CLOSED

Four events greatly affected the Scripture at the end of the Middle Ages.

1. **Chapters and verses.** Who knew? Around AD 300, Bible scholars began emerging as a profession. They tried numerous methods to organize the Scripture for easier reference in their writings, sermons, and correspondence. But not until the early thirteenth century did the Scripture receive the **chapter divisions** we know today, the work of Englishman **Stephen Langton.** He served as the archbishop of Canterbury (when the pope wasn't calling him to Rome or exiling him to France). His following of scholars probably helped with the work. The **verse designations** we use today were created by **Robert Estienne**, a famous French printer also known by the Latin name Stephanus. The first appearance of the chapters and verses together in one readable Bible was in his 1565 Bible.

2. **The invention of the ages: the Gutenberg printing press**! The first book printed with his new press and ink formulation was the Bible, in 1453 to 1455. Gutenberg made one hundred fifty to one hundred eighty copies of the Bible, each in two volumes, requiring a few years for the process. They came off the press in large sheets intended to be folded into pages. Some of these were sent to various artists to be illuminated at great time and expense, and were placed in covers of equal magnificence. Of course, these were in Latin and very costly. Those Bibles were placed in churches, libraries, and in wealthy homes. Some of these treasures survive still, mostly in museums. Today, in Museum of the Bible in Washington, DC, you can see a

model of what his press may have looked like—operated by staff so you can even see it in action.

3. **Paper!** Now here is something we take for granted today. The centuries-long Chinese monopoly on paper could not last forever. Paper began to be made in Europe near the end of the Middle Ages. Texts of all kinds began circulating widely, including the Bible. Some of the Gutenberg Bibles were even printed on paper. Much cheaper than parchment, paper enabled the population of this era to become increasingly literate through book production.

4. **The learning of East and West.** In 1453, Islamic armies conquered the city of Constantinople, forcing the Greek scholars of the Bible to flee west to Rome and elsewhere, and with them came the ancient manuscripts of the eastern churches. This confluence of scholarship traditions was just in time. With the combined knowledge of both East and West, scholars polished up the form and translation of Scripture after its long protection (and occasionally minor miscopying) in monasteries and churches all over Christendom.

THE PEOPLE MADE READY

While describing an English reformer in *Wolf Hall,* the first of her historical fiction trilogy, Hilary Mantel describes the rising hunger of the church for God's Word.

> As the word of God spreads, the people's eyes are opened to new truths. Until now . . . they knew Noah and the Flood, but not St. Paul. They could count over the sorrows of our Blessed Mother, and say how the damned are carried down to Hell. But they did not know the manifold miracles and sayings of Christ, nor the words and deeds of the apostles, simple men who, like the poor of London, pursued simple wordless trades. The story is much bigger that they ever thought it was.... You cannot tell people just part of the tale and then stop, or just tell the parts you choose. They have seen their religion painted on the walls of churches, or carved in stone, but now God's pen is poised, and he is ready to write his words in the books of their hearts. (p. 478)

We would have to be blind not to see the holy hand of God in this lead-up to the next century—**the Reformation**! Although idealized in so many ways, **reality says much more both positive and negative**.

The totalitarian grip of the Roman Church was loosed and, in the process, new churches arose preaching in the **vernacular of the people**.

But this did not occur overnight. **Fights** between the newly coined Protestants and the established churchmen of Rome gave political opportunity to the rising nationalism, and **bloody wars ensued**. None were spared the feverish eye of **heretic hunting**; many were burned at the stake, drawn and quartered, tortured, and beheaded. Even Wycliff's bones were dug up so they could be burned.

But the entirety of the Scripture, the whole counsel of God, was opened up. The Scripture would be restored to Christians and the rest of the world—**accessible, affordable, and readable**.

CHAPTER 4

THE REFORMATION TO 1850

LIFE AND DEATH

WHEN WE THINK OF THE PROTESTANT REFORMATION HISTORICALLY, we picture Martin Luther on October 31, 1517, dramatically nailing his ninety-five theses to the Castle Church door in Wittenberg. But the Reformation had been fomenting for a hundred years or more.

Before the Reformation, the Bible had been translated into several European languages without interference from the authorities in Rome who did not perceive a threat (at that time). Bibles in French, German, Italian, and other vernaculars were available, but literacy and cost remained a factor in these places, obstructing access to Scripture by the populace at large.

FOMENT

Christians were becoming restless, and society at large realized they were being shut out of understanding and reading the Bible. They were also disillusioned by the inability of the church against Europe's repeated waves of death from the Plague. The evident greed and corruption in the church eroded the respect and loyalty of the populace.

The first edition which Luther nailed to the door was in Latin, and there was little response. But general literacy had become more common by the sixteenth century. A middle class was taking form which demanded more understanding of their faith. When the ninety-five theses were posted in the common language, a firestorm erupted.

Latin Bibles and sermons in Latin were not satisfying. Many previous movements sought to teach Christians from the Bible, such as Jan Hus, Savonarola, and the Waldensians. Such movement leaders were violently shut down by the leaders of the Roman Church, deeply entwined with secular authorities.

Thus a new and exciting stage for the Bible was set: printers who had sixty years of experience! Affordable paper was now produced in Europe. Additionally, Greek language scholars had flooded in after the Ottoman Turk takeover of Constantinople. With their western European counterparts, they dug into comparing Greek texts of the New Testament. These students of Scripture were **polishing the precious jewel with more accuracy**, just as civilization was coming out of the Middle Ages.

The world was opening up to the age of exploration as well, starting with Columbus in 1492. The age of worldwide European colonization was begun. Despite their egregious mistreatment of the natives, and the resulting hindrances erected to faith in Jesus, wherever they went the Bible went with them. Now was the time! Europe was the place! Martin Luther was the first survivor of many!

THE AGE OF PRESERVATION

The new influx of **Greek language scholar**s from the East added to a long-standing tradition of honor for Scripture. For the thousand years of the Middle Ages, the Bible and particularly the New Testament had been copied by monks in monasteries, or by scribes in scriptoriums. Much evidence shows that they gave their best efforts to the job, and the Bible weathered its Dark Ages of isolation very well. It is indeed very remarkable—a standing tribute to these diligent monks and scribes.

BIBLE TRANSLATION INTO THE VERNACULAR

A big thrust of the Reformation was giving people a translation of the Bible in their own language—that is, the vernacular. Thanks to his good knowledge of Greek, the original language of the New Testament, Luther's translation into German was very well done. Other European countries followed suit until almost every country from the Roman Empire of late antiquity had a Bible in their own language.

However, the church and the government were so intertwined that together they enforced and condoned capital punishment. William Tyndale, a famous English Bible translator and reformer in the 1520s, fled persecution to the

European continent, where he translated the Bible into the English language. His editions came in *quarto* and *octo* sizes, which could be held by hand like our Bibles today. They were illegal at the time, so their small size also helped them to be hidden easily. People were eager to read the Bible for themselves—despite the threat of a death penalty for having one—so printed Bibles flew off the shelves.

After Henry VIII's famous separation from the Roman Church in 1527, the Bible became legal in England. The king authorized a translation under his own auspices, the Great Bible. However, Tyndale's Bible remained the best English translation in the sixteenth century. Despite this, and possibly because of it, Tyndale was betrayed by a so-called friend and martyred by the Roman Church authorities in 1536.

ENGLISH BIBLES IN A NUTSHELL

During the Reformation, the Bible took on the shape and appearance we know today, and like today, a variety in format arose among countries and languages. Size and shape differed, with both larger and smaller Bibles. Their varying placement also had an influence. The church Bibles were certainly very large, designed to rest on stands and pulpits rather than personal daily use. Some individuals owned smaller Bibles they could read, at a lower cost.

Hunger for Scripture arose in English churches. Sometimes the Great Bible would be chained in a church to prevent its theft. And while the homily was being preached in Latin from the pulpit in front, others would read the Great Bible to the people crowding around in the back. In some churches, this was occurring simultaneously with six Bibles placed throughout the sanctuary. It was noted that often the noise drowned out the preacher or priest in front. Thus, England would become the country that led Europe—and eventually the world —in translating, printing, polishing, and distributing the jewel of Scripture.

What a picture of the Reformation and the people's hunger for the Bible!

Not all were of the excellence of Luther and Tyndale. Many scholars of the sixteenth century decried the condition of the Greek manuscripts available to them after the Middle Ages.

THE GREEK TEXT

The Hebrew Old Testament was very protected, copied by Jews over the centuries. It remains fully intact to this day with little error. But with the New Testament written in the Greek language, **influential accents and declensions** could be miscopied. Thus, discrepancies were reproduced through hand-copying. The differing strokes were copied into subsequent copies. Something like family lines of texts developed, as the unique strokes on one miscopied manuscript characterized all following copies of that manuscript. The Latin New Testament texts also carried transcription problems over the centuries.

The differences between the hand-copied texts were largely minor. For instance, words could be misspelled. Copyists' talent for accuracy could differ. There were no erasers for parchment, so if a verse was accidentally repeated, it was left in place to avoid an ugly scratch-out. Notes placed in the margin by one copyist would be misunderstood by the next copyist as a verse that should have been inserted.

Thus, this precious jewel of God's Word was in need of polishing to restore its original luster.

ERASMUS

One such scholar, the great Greek scholar and teacher known as Erasmus, polished the text of the Greek New Testament using the limited manuscripts then available. He was there at just the right time, when the Bible was emerging from its hibernation during the Middle Ages.

The life of Erasmus was contemporaneous with Martin Luther; however, Erasmus was a Roman Catholic teacher and remained so, never serving as a parish priest. How he managed to remain a noted Greek scholar and avoid Catholic persecution must have made for an interesting life. How did he survive? Not functioning as a priest perhaps spared him some direct accountability. Other contributing factors: his winsome (though at times confrontational) personality, radar for trouble, and political instincts.

Erasmus set the tone for the Greek New Testament by comparing the manuscripts available to him, and identifying the text most likely to be accurate. His final Greek text, known as *Textus Receptus* ("The Received Text"), was published in 1535 and with his revisions was used by translators for several hundred years.

There was obvious protection over the Scripture because no major doctrine was damaged by these minor glitches. **None of the essential message or text of the Bible was harmed** in any way by the centuries of copyists. The Bible was then, and is today, **as intact as it ever was**. The need for polishing was not a detriment but rather a tribute to this remarkable treasure. Many thousands of man-hours have gone into this polishing effort, and made it the **best text it can be today**.

Gospel of Mark with marginal comments (arrows added). https://en.
wikipedia.org/wiki/Minuscule_4, from National Library of France

THE KING JAMES BIBLE

This Bible was ordered into production by King James I of England in 1604.
Committees of biblical scholars with individual assignments were appointed,
who worked from the *Textus Receptus* of 1525 and other relevant texts available
in the sixteenth century. Finally, their translation hit the presses in 1611 and the
rest is history.

This Bible translation arose from dissatisfaction with the two English-
language Bibles then popular: the Geneva Bible (with its heavy Puritan, anti-
Catholic notes) and the Bishops' Bible (perceived as out of date). The original

King James Bible was **revised for grammar, punctuation and spelling in 1769** and became the King James Version we now read today. It became the most widely read and preached English version of that day, and remained so until the nineteenth century.

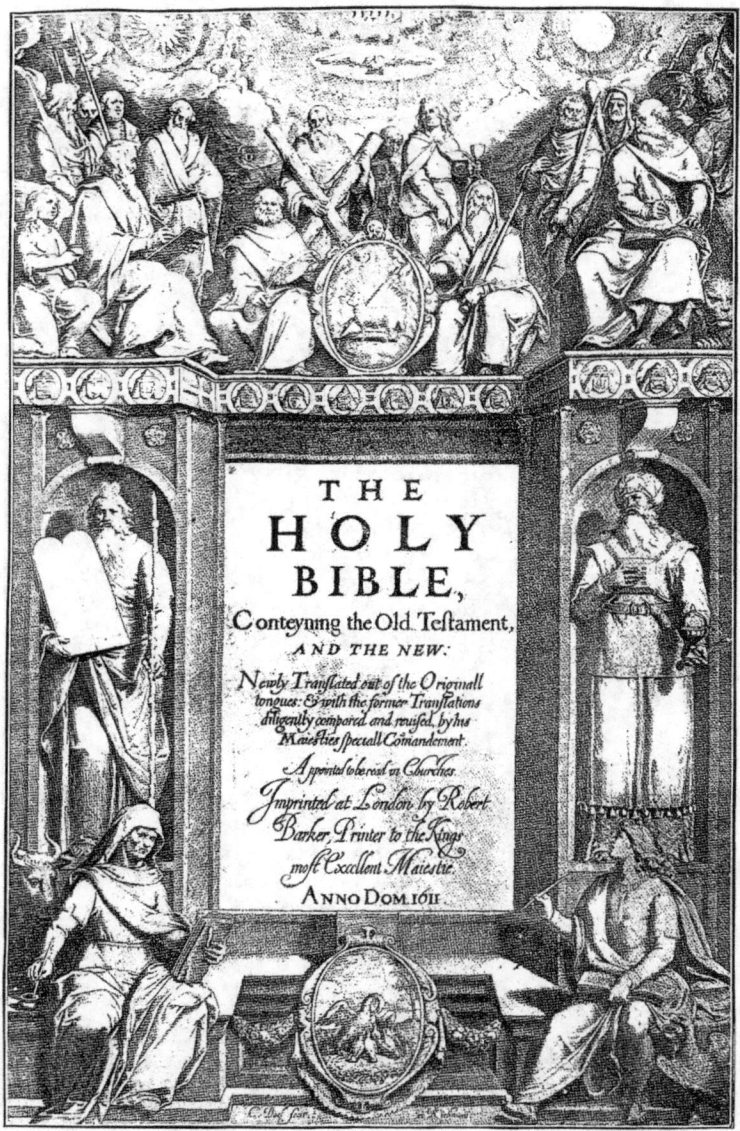

Title page of original printed King James Bible. (William P. Pearce. *The World's Best Book and the Best Book for the World*. Pacific Press Publishing Assoc., 1931, p. 2.)

The King James Bible, then called the Authorized Version, came at an interesting point in the history of the English language. Its lofty wording and lovely sound fit the literary style of the time in England, used by Shakespeare and John Milton (the author of *Paradise Lost* and other works). So beautiful and popular was it that many idioms in our language today come from it, such as Job's "the skin of my teeth" and the Psalms' "apple of my eye." Indeed it is hard for me to hear the Twenty-Third Psalm in any other version! "Because the Lord is my shepherd; I have everything that I need" just doesn't have the same ring as "The Lord is my shepherd; I shall not want."

A WORD ABOUT ENGLAND

For good and for ill, Western Europe became a launching point for New World explorers and colonizers, but the people of England led the world with their intense interest in biblical scholarship. England became the center for the distribution and updating of the Bible. We could say that England had a heart to polish and spread the Bible around the world, with the United States soon following.

ENTER THE BIBLE SOCIETIES

In the 1770s, Bible societies had been formed in England and France to distribute Bibles to soldiers and seamen. Then in 1804, the British and Foreign Bible Society (BFBS) was quietly formed by a group of Christians passionate that everyone in Wales could have an affordable, readable Bible in their own language.

The Bible societies grew in focus and influence, and the rest is history. It is hard to exaggerate the impact of this organization and its offshoots upon the Bible and Christian faith around the world.

The BFBS maintained its clear vision through many challenging times. They were (and still are) committed to welcoming all Christian churches to participate in the leadership and distribution of Bibles, as described on their website:

We believe the Bible is God's gift to the world. We want everyone to discover its message for themselves.

Because of that, we translate the Bible and make it accessible in people's heart languages. We bring it into public spaces where its voice can be heard, for instance through the National Parliamentary Prayer Breakfast or *The Pitch* film fund. We tell its stories, for instance through the Open the Book programme with primary-age children. We encourage people who've never thought the Bible was for them to explore it for themselves, and see life through a different lens. (Bible Society, 2025. https://www. biblesociety.org.uk/about-us/our-work/)

The BFBS encouraged many to form their own Bible societies, in both countries and organizations around the world. Instead of becoming territorial, they became the essence of the opposite, freely welcoming—as they still do—the help of anyone who adheres to their goals. Together, the Bible societies rejoiced in the success and help of their partners. When any resistance to the work arose, the BFBS helped work it out.

In addition, the Bibles they distributed, both at the beginning and today, are not marked with any notes and do not favor any particular faith or church. It's just the Bible. Because of their work, we can easily find an affordable, readable Bible in most languages. Working with missionaries, churches, and Bible translators, the BFBS and its offshoots are seeing to it that Jesus' statement is fulfilled:

And this gospel of the kingdom will be preached in the whole world as a testimony to all nations, and then the end will come. (Matthew 24:14)

POLISHING THE JEWEL

By producing his *Textus Receptus* of the Greek New Testament, Erasmus became the first Reformer to practice textual criticism (better called textual analysis). This branch of biblical research seeks the most accurate text in the original languages of the Bible, particularly the New Testament. An exact match is impossible to verify, since **the originals are no longer extant**. Textual critics analyze verse by verse, manuscript by manuscript, to identify which text provides the best rendering to approximate the originals written by the New Testament authors.

Their valuable effort gives us the best Greek New Testament from which to translate the Bible into the languages of the world. This was and is no small challenge. Scholars endowed with the interest, devotion, and gifts to endure this meticulous analysis spend years producing the best Greek text for this beloved book.

One of the first such scholars had been Jerome (AD c. 347-420), who found the best Greek and Hebrew texts at that time to produce his translation into Latin. Meanwhile, the Eastern church produced centuries of Greek scholars whose 1453 escape from Constantinople to the West united them with scholars like Erasmus.

Erasmus gave his best, working with the Greek manuscripts available at the time. But those sources were superseded by the work of later scholars. Principles for identifying the most likely original text were developed in the sixteenth and seventeenth centuries by textual critic John Mill and others. Archaeologists contributed much as well, especially their discoveries of **more ancient Greek manuscripts** during the eighteenth and nineteenth centuries.

In 1881, two scholars named Westcott and Hort produced an updated text of the Greek New Testament which incorporated these great strides in textual analysis over the previous three hundred years. With their work, a new version of the English Bible was produced, the Revised Version of 1881 and 1886. While it lacked in the sonorous language of the King James Version, it was a big hit for its accuracy, relying on the best textual sources then available.

MANUSCRIPT COLLECTION

The first step in creating the best and closest to the Greek text was the collection of ancient manuscripts. The first to be identified was the great codex held in the Vatican Library since at least 1481 (and probably much earlier), thus named *Vaticanus*. It was dated around AD 350 and contained much of the Old and the New Testament in uncial (large) Greek letters on fine vellum parchment.

During its exciting history, the Vaticanus manuscript was captured by Napoleon and brought to Paris. After its return to the Vatican, it was available a few times to scholars, but the trek to Rome and the guarded nature of its librarians discouraged access to this codex. It remained fairly inaccessible for centuries.

The next important ancient codex collected was *Alexandrinus*. This codex was given to England by the Eastern church in 1627 and placed in the British Museum where it resides to this day. Containing most of the Greek Bible, the Alexandrinus codex is dated about AD 450, and was the first such ancient codex to become readily available to scholars.

The arrival of the Alexandrinus codex sparked the hunt in earnest for similar ancient codices. Codex *Bezae* was a Greek and Latin parallel with the Gospels and Acts, produced in the fifth century. Codex *Claromontanus* was another Latin/Greek parallel, containing the Pauline Epistles of the sixth century. After their discovery, these codices became available for study in Paris.

And so, for two hundred years, the **collection of ancient manuscripts** continued apace. It's inspiring that **over five thousand artifacts from antiquity**, from complete Bibles to fragments, have been rediscovered and preserved for textual analysis.

English scholars did not immediately embrace the principles of textual criticism, nor revisions to the Greek text of the Bible, but the seeds were sown. Meanwhile, the manuscripts were collected which would eventually bring increasing agreement among scholars.

TISCHENDORF

By the nineteenth century, the time had come for the Bible to get its **millennial clean-up**. During this time a man of great biblical knowledge and amazing energy did much for the Bible's text, and showed an example for others to follow.

Constantine Tischendorf found one of the most important ancient codices in a monastery on Mount Sinai. He dramatically stopped it from being used as kindling, casually burned by the monks! Next, he oversaw its preservation in Russia for scholars to study. Sold to England later in the twentieth century and named *Sinaiticus*, its origin dates from approximately AD 325. Sinaiticus joined Vaticanus and Alexandrinus as the **three most important codices** used in textual analysis. It now resides in the British Museum, along with Alexandrinus.

Page of Codex Vaticanus. (William P. Pearce. *The World's Best Book and the Best Book for the World.* Pacific Press Publishing Assoc., 1931, p. 88.)

THE AGE OF PLENTY

To date, there are about **five thousand pieces of ancient biblical materials** to study, thanks to the diligence of thousands of devoted people like Tischendorf. Some of these materials are mere fragments; others are almost entire texts of the Bible. Most are of very ancient character.

The big three codices date from AD 325 to 450. In comparison, full copies of most books from antiquity are no more recent than AD 1000. Works such as Julius Caesar's writings, or Homer's *Iliad* and *Odyssey,* barely survived antiquity, with no early forms in existence whereas **the Bible has an abundance**.

Scholars have developed a hierarchy of importance regarding the texts they use in biblical analysis. The first are the big three, called the Witnesses, which we'll come back to. Following closely after them are other manuscripts of ancient origins, including some very ancient translations not Greek, such as **the Syriac**. Less ancient documents are also utilized, which may shed light on a particular verse.

THE PERIOD REVIEWED

The Bible became the important project for scholars, merchants, and rulers; it remained so for several hundred years. Many countries were satisfied with their Bible in the native language, but England kept going for improvement in their translations.

When the psychopathic King Henry VIII declared freedom from Roman Catholicism, the side effect for the Bible was his dictate of an English Bible for the people in every church. Bible translations soon became available for every sect. For instance, the ultra-Calvinists had their Geneva Bible with their anti-Catholic notes. Merchants accelerated the spread of the Scripture, as they bought and resold the expanding number of Bible editions.

Whereas the key word for the previous chapter could be dark, the key word for this chapter has to be weird. What with the newly minted Protestants fighting with old school Catholics, and many burning at the stake for their beliefs, plus the evils of the Spanish Inquisition, the Bible's world was in turmoil.

While the printing press and paper spread many new ideas and encouraged literacy across the known world, the explorers and conquistadors headed for the unknown. They established Western European colonies. Tragically, the explorers traded diseases with the indigenous people, whom they often treated cruelly. Such a bad start likely caused years of delay in establishing biblical churches in the New World.

Yet amid that, the gospel spread along with the Bible, bringing our review to 1850 and the advent of a period I call the "**Great Bifurcation**."

CHAPTER 5

1850 TO THE PRESENT

THE GREAT BIFURCATION AND BEYOND

THE EVENTS AND PATTERNS I'M DESCRIBING DID NOT START OR STOP exactly in any one year, as usual in records of history—but it conveniently signifies a distinct *before* and *after*.

Bibles in 1800 were far more available than in previous centuries. Advances in paper production and in printing had reduced the cost; shipping and transportation brought Bibles to most of the colonized and settled world. This was the era of the large family Bible; few people carried a Bible. Curiously, by the 1860s, American Civil War soldiers carried pocket Bibles—some of which stopped ricocheted bullets!

When the nineteenth century began, the Bible enjoyed respect throughout Western civilization (although not everyone lived by it). In culture, as in religion, the providence of God was an acknowledged reality.

Yet by 1850, **two divergent directions** were becoming firmly rooted throughout society. The first: active **disrespect** for Scripture. The second was passion for its **polishing and promulgation, with general respect for God's providence**.

The Bible came to inhabit two very different universes—parallel universes. In one universe, the Bible traveled the world, and many languages graced its pages. In the other universe, it was being picked apart: its credibility, accuracy, and authority were not merely questioned, but absolutely denied by many influential leaders and scholars.

What divided the universal regard for God's Word? To see what happened, it helps to fast forward from 1800 to 1985—to see an **outlandish outcome** of the disrespect universe.

YOU CAN'T MAKE THIS UP

In 1985, an effort began which truly demands two cliches: "You can't make this stuff up" and "Truth is stranger than fiction."

That effort was the so-called Jesus Seminar! Sounds interesting, right?

In 1985, Dr. Robert Funk, a professor with a weak view of the Bible's integrity, founded a think tank at the Westar Institute, and invited others of like mind to join his Jesus Seminar. Its stated goal? To examine the Gospels and decide what Jesus actually said! They thought they had some magical insight and could reliably judge what Jesus did and did not say.

Dr. Funk hand-picked about fifty academics; others of varying academic stature brought the number to about two hundred. Indeed, many of these "Fellows of the Institute" were not qualified scholars, but so what? The stated goal presumed an open mind, but that clearly was not the case. Instead, the fix was in.

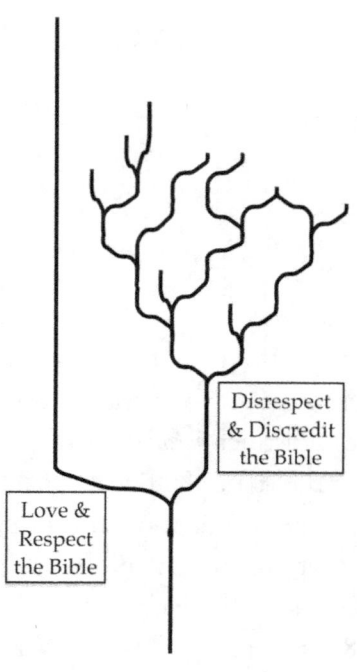

The Great Bifurcation

These Fellows had yearly scheduled meetings to examine what Jesus said, and vote on the accuracy of His words. Did they discuss, confer, come to consensus, or publish opinions in reputable journals? In normal academic seminars, that's the protocol, but not these Fellows. They voted anonymously with colored beads placed in a jar. No joke!

This entire process should have been laughed off the academic planet, but that would have been politically incorrect. **Many academics were afraid to question such craziness.**

Here's what each bead vote meant:

Red bead = Jesus did say.
Pink Bead = Jesus may have said.
Grey bead = Jesus probably did not say.
Black bead = Jesus did not say.

Didn't I tell you? You can't make this stuff up.

Besides the four biblical Gospels, they added the spurious Gospel of Thomas to their source cache. This extra manuscript was found in Egypt alongside other Gnostic writings and has long been discredited as including real sayings of Jesus. This is especially because of its late composition in about AD 340. Early in the Jesus Seminar process, they black-beaded most of the Gospel of John, leaving them with only the Synoptic Gospels and Thomas. But so what? It suited their purpose.

Ballot box with beads. (Image courtesy of Massachusetts Historical Society)

At the end of this farce, the Fellows published papers, wrote books, and even published their own so-called "new testament" which they named The Scholars Version! Later, however, they did publish some of their so-called findings in their own press.

All of this mostly fizzled out for lack of interest, after the founder of Westar died in 2005.

What did they conclude that Jesus actually said? Only a few verses could be considered genuine, which were politically correct for our time. So, maybe the real purpose of all of this was to join the clamor to discredit the Bible.

DOWNSHIFT TO DISRESPECT

How did this universe of disrespect for the Bible develop? How did we get from widespread respect for the Bible and the providence of God, to the 1980s Jesus Seminar, the Fellows of which set themselves up as judges of Scripture?

Since 1700, a disbelief in Scripture's integrity arose in Western theology. The so-called scholars of the Enlightenment applied humanism, reason, and Darwinism to their study of the Old Testament. This practice was called higher criticism, and the outcome was no surprise. They concluded that some of the Old Testament was profoundly edited about 400 BC, or even earlier. Such extensive editing is called **redacting**; those who do it are called **redactors**.

Hidden within academia were little pockets of doubt about the authorship of the Torah from the 1600s onward. But only around 1850 did these minority opinions gain widespread traction in **colleges and seminaries**, which then filtered them into Western culture as credible opinions and even likely fact. Any geographic region with a university in its vicinity was affected by the disease of unquestioned disrespect.

A major challenge to the Bible's integrity came from Germany, called the Wellhausen-Graf Hypothesis. It proposed that several ancient editors had edited the Pentateuch—so thoroughly, in fact, that Moses did not even write it. These ancient editors were designated the Jahwist, the Elohim, Priestly, and Deuteronomist. As this theory developed, it became called the Documentary Hypothesis, with the nickname JEDP, after those four supposed groups.

Despite the many archeological discoveries that support the truth of the Scripture as it is written, this seriously flawed grid remained the norm.

Only recently has **the theory begun losing its grip** on academic and pastoral thinking worldwide, as are many other outlandish theories. You'll see why ridiculous beliefs are necessary to justify the Documentary Hypothesis.

FLAWED LEADER TRAINING

Many seminaries and even **Ivy League colleges** in the US were founded by those who held the Bible as sacred. These institutions had trained pastors and missionaries in the Scripture since their founding. But many of these same institutions and their professors took on the so-called new ideas, while those who voiced the long-proven integrity of Scripture were penalized and even became afraid to speak out in fear of losing their academic positions. Such bullying and fear is entering many arenas in our time; the more things change, the more they stay the same.

Over the years, this theory took over, like a drop of dark ink takes over a bucket of water and changes the entire color. Despite its many **flaws and contradictions**, the Documentary Hypothesis infiltrated the seminaries which train many pastors. They joined in casting doubt on the veracity of the Bible. The unique pressures upon the academic professions became a swell of uniformity, penalizing the careers of any who held to the integrity of the Bible.

As a result, they turned out many pastors without solid biblical (or any) foundations, still leading churches today. I have always wondered—if a person doesn't believe the Bible, why be a pastor at all? New seminaries formed to counteract this academic skepticism and have produced solid biblical pastors for certain denominations.

This is where we find ourselves—seeing churches and denominations divided, whether or not to uphold the classic orthodox beliefs presented in Scripture.

An aside: While discussing the Jesus Seminar with a 1970s graduate of an elite college, he said his liberal religion professor had written his own gospel with Jesus and the apostles as Eskimos (as native Alaskans were then called)—**questioned by no one except the student**.

Jesus the Eskimo?! (Image generated by ChatGPT, OpenAI, 2025.)

SCRIPTURE REJECTED— FALSEHOODS WELCOMED

Besides the above major movement which eroded trust in the Bible, other movements arose as well: Transcendentalism (persons can be spiritual without the Bible), Darwinism (the events in Genesis are false), Postmodernism (words themselves are untrustworthy), and Freudianism (it's all about the subconscious and libido). These and many other false beliefs added to the slide toward skepticism. **Yet, one after another, they each show little staying power over the years**.

The French philosopher Voltaire was a leading skeptic known for writing the satire *Candide* in 1759. Henrietta Mears in *A Look at the Old Testament* likened such men to Judah's King Jehoaikim, who sliced and burned the scroll of Jeremiah's prophecy.

How many, like the atheist Voltaire, have taken the penknife of their intellect and have cut to pieces God's Word. They think by destroying the Bible they can do away with its power. (p. 189)

These theories were and are intended to shake the foundation and veracity of both the Old and New Testaments. From **academia and churches**, the disrespect for the Bible permeated much of culture. Even though many scholars of repute in diverse fields upheld the Scripture, despite people all over the world believing the Scripture, a great skepticism about its authority, accuracy, and authenticity remains a barrier today—and may even affect you, dear reader.

If you want to enjoy our faith in God from the Bible, you must overcome these barriers. And this is a central point of this book—to give you the knowledge of the true and the false. **You can overcome the subtle voices which say that the Bible is based on lies**. No competing explanation has had the staying power that the Bible has demonstrated.

REDACTORS AND MULTIPLE AUTHORS

Advocates of the Documentary Hypothesis say that editors, called *redactors*, changed the Torah multiple times over centuries for the entire Jewish community. They say this editing occurred at various times in Israel's history, especially after the Jews' return to Jerusalem from captivity. The supposed editors even changed the names of God from Yahweh to Elohim to Adonai, and altered names to suit their times. These theoretical editors virtually rewrote the Torah.

Mimicking the presuppositions of the Documentary Hypothesis, other Bible books are said to be redacted products influenced by multiple authors—even Isaiah's prophecy. Similar *multiple authorship* theories are advanced about the Writings and the Prophets, the other two divisions comprising the Old Testament with the Torah. The **theories** all share a common idea: that unnamed Jewish editors significantly altered what was written and handed down.

Even Jesus' references to the words of Moses are called into question, because these theories hold that Moses did not write Torah. Faith in the truth of the Old Testament is shaken. All integrity of the Bible is in doubt.

REDACTION THEORY

Redaction means pervasive and invasive editing, moving content to different places, eliminating material deemed undesirable, and inserting content deemed more currently relevant. The editors responsible are called redactors.

Put it this way: The theory requires that the Bible, as the Jews knew it in 400 BC, was available for a complete overhaul by unknown people. In modern times, we might call it cutting and pasting followed by republication of a new edition.

A very redacted document can bear little resemblance to the original. To redact an ancient beloved document requires three judgments: 1) insufficiency in the original, 2) qualities more pleasing in the culture and time of the redactor, and 3) unified receptivity among all who hold the former document dear.

REFUTING REDACTION

Why is the Documentary Hypothesis—a.k.a. JEDP—so **unlikely to be true**? How do we argue against JEDP and similar theories of multiple authorship? The Jewish mentality of those days is evident in the care shown by Ezra and the returnees. The Scripture was **ingrained into their hearts and minds and lives**. The books of the Law, the Writings, and Prophets were too sacred and too protected to suffer such desecration.

Despite Israel's rebellions and idolatries, those of the faithful remnant were steeped in their Book. Those Levites, priests, elders, and prophets had memorized large portions of the Torah and taught the people from it for centuries, up to today in our literate time. So internalized was the Torah in the Jews that the redaction of Scripture cannot be true. Changes in these scrolls would never escape scrutiny; such redaction would never be permitted.

The realities of publication combine with Jewish ways of heart, mind, and history to provide powerful refutations for redaction theories.

1. Impractical: too many copies to replace.
2. Unmanageable: no hierarchical control.
3. Unopposed: no evidence of the expected controversy.
4. Rigid names: permitting only one name for God.
5. Static styles: requiring an author to write the same way all the time.

IMPRACTICAL

During their exile, the Jews recognized the importance of the holy Scriptures, and copied them assiduously. Soon the scrolls were widely dispersed. When the JEDP theorists had their supposed redactors at work, Jewish synagogues with their scrolls had spread throughout the ancient world, in the Diaspora. Was a massive movement begun to replace the old Torah with the new? Or was it sneaky, one synagogue at a time?

Would it be possible to redact all of these scattered copies? Of course not. If redactions were issued, they would come from a central headquarters of scribes and priests, publishing a worldwide dictate to replace the old copies with the so-called new and improved redaction. Then every Jewish synagogue would have to comply, if the Documentary Hypothesis is to be true.

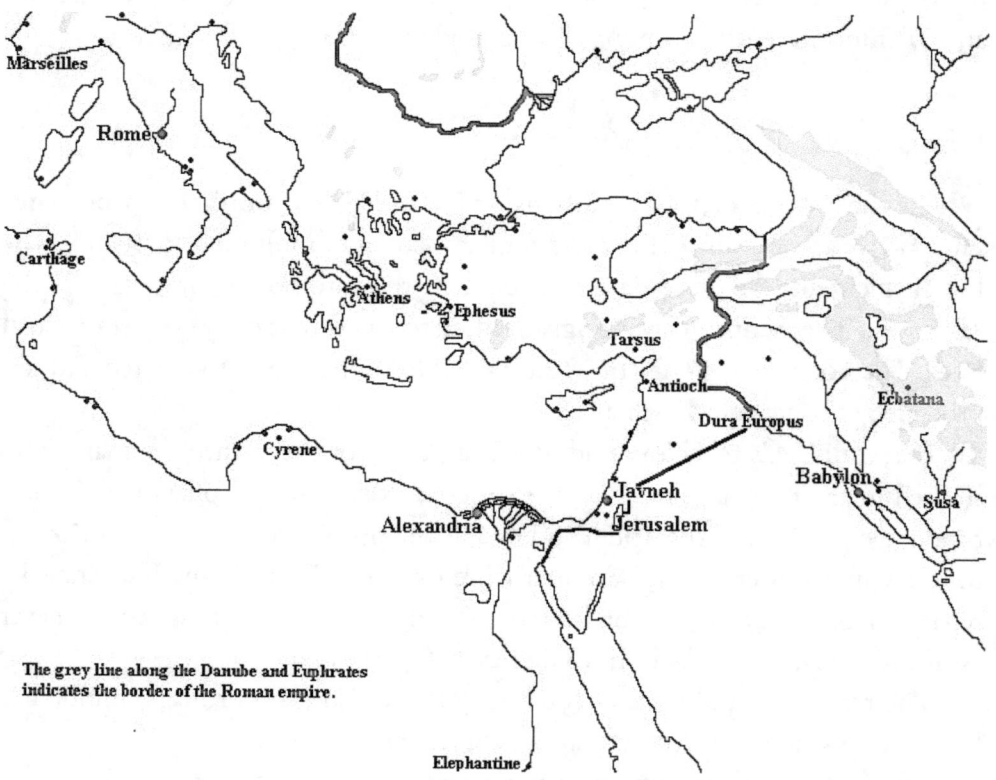

Jewish communities of the Diaspora in the first century AD. (Johan Lendering, "Origins of the Dispersion." Livius.org, 2020.)

UNMANAGEABLE

For this hypothetical redaction to succeed would require a strong centralized grip on every synagogue among the dispersed Jews. How strong a grip? Redaction theory fancifully requires that no Jews would keep their old Torah, but permit its destruction. Yet no evidence exists that such a centralized hierarchy existed in post-exile Judaism, nor that any Jewish settlement complied.

Experience with the **power of religious tradition** proves that religious people would disagree. Suppose some progressive synagogues relished the so-called new Torah and gave up the outdated Torah. Others would be devotees of the old Torah and defend it, lambasting the bastardized Torah. As a result, history would show two greatly different versions of Torah in circulation ever since. This has never happened.

After the redaction department released its new version, at least two Torahs would emerge. That would be the minimum, assuming that all the editors simultaneously cooperated to present one revised consensus edition. But the Documentary Hypothesis says the redaction occurred in several stages. Even if the editing had been quiet and secretive, there would be historical evidence of three or four substantially different Torahs.

UNOPPOSED

Because of the protection afforded the holy books, even during bad times, no such redaction or editing of Scripture could have succeeded—especially not during the hot mess of the intertestamental period. Instead of compliance would be **outcry**. Such a replacement effort by the redactors would have caused a controversy heard and published all around the known world, just as it would today. Yet none exists—not even a peep. Josephus, the exhaustive, detail-oriented Jewish historian of the first century, never mentions such a thing.

RIGID NAMES

Supporters of the multiple-authorship theories rely on the variety of names, styles, and points of reference. Consider the different names of God used in the Torah. The Documentary Hypothesis attributes each name to the preferences of unique redactors. But in fact, the common practice of the ancient religions was multiple names for their gods. We do the same today; an example is the long-beloved poster showing all of God's Bible names. To interpret that as evidence of many fingers in the pie is a pitiful disdain for the Bible.

The Old Testament does have an important distinction in the matter of the divine names. God's names are all qualities of His character or being. Far from arbitrary or popular names, they express facets of His Person. In contrast, people named their pagan divinities by the aspect of life they thought to control: rain, childbirth, wars, crops, geographical settings, and other day-to-day vagaries.

STATIC STYLES

The advocates also point to varying styles as evidence of multiple authors. They reason that an author is limited to one style and one set of preferences which will not change. But even modern authors use a variety of styles. To judge the ancient

Bible documents by such an arbitrary and unrealistic standard reveals that disrespect is the foregone conclusion.

Over their long history, God's people were called variously Hebrews, Children of Israel, Israelites, and Jews. By any name, they were always People of the Book. Their Book grew through their history, ultimately including the Torah, the Writings, and the Prophets. Many of the components were composed over decades. To suppose that no writer could develop in his style is ludicrous and unrealistic.

Clayton Howard Ford thoroughly demolished this error in his book *Who Really Wrote the Bible? A Response to the Documentary Hypothesis*. Ford points out that writers through the ages have used different styles at will—and still do. Ancient writers freely used scribes to help write their words—adding another style as a result—with no thought of what we call plagiarism today.

JEDP IS DEAD

There is **no evidence** supporting any of these necessary beliefs for the multiple authorship theories. At no time in Jewish history was there more than one Torah, and certainly not two or more Torahs. Remember, these religious and cultural **documents were very public**. They carried great weight and strict legal authority in their civil society. These writings were imbued with centuries of love and respect, indeed obedience, by many millions of Jewish people. **Two or more Torahs could not coexist**. Outrage over such an attempt would surely come to light. Many Jews would expose the effort. A conspiracy of this magnitude could not be hidden.

What possibly motivates these JEDP theorists? Plenty of motive now exists: to be recognized as a modern scholar by discrediting the Bible or demoting Scripture to merely one among many writings thought sacred.

So, with these refutations in mind, dear reader, if you gave any credence to the Documentary Hypothesis, please rethink it! Its flaws are becoming more widely recognized. Like the philosophies *du jour* mentioned earlier, deconstruction is losing its grip. **The fervor once used to defend the theory and its many handicaps is now waning**.

PASSION FOR DISCOVERY

Even as disrespect grew, in the other universe a passion for Scripture grew simultaneously. In chapter four we saw the beginning of polishing the jewel—the

Greek Bible manuscripts from which translations are made. Scripture went from handwritten manuscripts to machine printed in the late 1500s. As careful as monks and scribes had been over the centuries, mostly small and inconsequential errors crept into the texts coming out of the Middle Ages.

The polishing from about 1500 to 1800 used the ancient texts then available. But questions remained, and the Bible needed further polishing. So, a quest for more ancient manuscripts ensued, and the following century fulfilled that quest.

From 1850 onward, scholars and adventurers scoured the Middle East and Europe, haunting the back alleys for more ancient manuscripts. They enjoyed great success, and discovered **many more ancient manuscripts** which shed light on the texts of the Bible. Many discoveries came at great personal cost to the finders.

REVISITING THE WITNESSES

The three codices described in the last chapter had great consequence: Vaticanus, Sinaiticus, and Alexandrinus. The family lines of each miscopied manuscript, reproducing the distinctive strokes, enables a manuscript genealogy to be reverse-constructed, just like the genetics of human family lines. Amid the many manuscripts discovered, these three became recognized for their position before the family lines of the differing texts. Scholars began to call them the "Witnesses," as they still do.

These three ancient texts do not look like any book we know. Written mostly on thin parchment, now fragile, darkened from age, with the ink faded, only a professional can read them. Yet they yield the most amazing knowledge of the Bible. With their invaluable help, today's texts of the Greek Bible are the most accurate, considering the originals are not available. The most widely accepted Greek text today is the Nestle-Aland for its accuracy.

Codex Sinaiticus was found in Saint Catherine's Monastery in Egypt in 1844. Through different routes, the bulk of it came to reside in the British Museum in London. At first, the text was only available to a few scholars, but over the years, through technology and photography, the text image is now accessible with permission. Sinaiticus includes all of the New Testament and some parts of the Old and some Apocryphal works. Its estimated age of AD 330–360 makes it one of the most important tools in the polishing of the jewel.

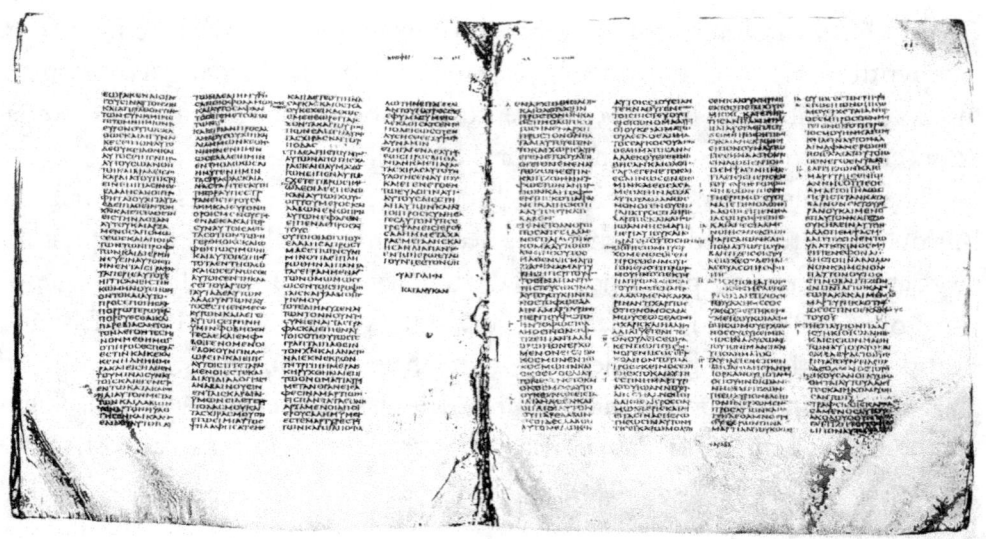

A two-page spread of the Codex Sinaiticus. (Image courtesy of the British Museum.)

Codex Vaticanus resides in the Vatican library in Rome and is considered the oldest of the three Witnesses, dated to AD 300–325. Unlike Sinaiticus, Vaticanus was housed in the library at least since the AD 1475 Vatican catalogue, and was probably there for many centuries before. It was largely kept from scholars until the 1800s. However, thanks to digital advancements and the openness of the Vatican, this ancient codex can now be used widely to research the text. This Witness lacks some parts of the New Testament, but is almost complete in the Old.

Codex Alexandrinus is named for its origin in Alexandria, Egypt, and journeyed to Constantinople then to the British Museum in the 1600s where it resides today. Dated AD 400–440, it was the first ancient witness used by biblical scholars to polish the jewel. It contains all but a few leaves of the Old Testament and the New Testament.

These three Witnesses are not alone, but simply the most complete ancient manuscripts. As such, they preceded the family lines which duplicated unique miscopied strokes and emendations. Today, **5,700 sources** are commonly recognized, from whole texts to fragments of the Greek and Latin Bible, in addition to **writings from early church fathers** containing quotes from Scripture. **Thanks to technology**, most of these sources are now available to study from anywhere in the world.

The originals are curated and preserved with the utmost care they deserve in libraries and other places of importance. We'll be delighted with discovery of more manuscripts and fragments in the future, both to confirm what has been found and to shed light on some unanswered questions. I think the Vatican Library has more to show us in the future.

While the universe of Bible passion grew, the universe of disrespect was developing as well.

WHY THE TWO UNIVERSES

Remember, about the mid-nineteenth century, burning the Bible was of no effect, because the Scripture was easily available and relatively affordable in most major languages and a few obscure ones. This fire of the Bible's worldwide span was lit and could not be stopped.

Neither was neglect very effective, because the Christian faith, along with the Bible, was enthusiastically taking root all over the world. Many individuals and churches worldwide held firmly to the veracity of the Bible, often at great expense to themselves.

So started the fresh attack described above: disrespect and discredit. That universe of activity by academia and beyond ran parallel to the worldwide distribution of the Bible and the attendant growth of the Christian faith.

THE OTHER UNIVERSE: RESPECT

In this parallel universe, the Bible was beloved and respected. For the first time since its compilation, it would now travel the entire globe. The start of this journey was small.

In chapter four, we reviewed the creation of **the Bible societies**. The first and most influential was the British and Foreign Bible Society (BFBS), formed in 1808. Its stated purpose was to provide Bibles, free or for a modest fee, to anyone who wanted one in their own language. At first it focused on Wales, but quickly became global as the British Empire grew.

We cannot overstate the profound impact these societies made. They were a spiritual phenomenon with permanent benefit for the life of the Bible. Rarely acknowledged for their work, their members committed to one goal—a readable Bible for everyone who wanted one. Soon after the BFBS started, the American Bible Society began in 1818, and shared the aim of the British and Foreign Bible Society. Hundreds of associate societies followed.

Over time, the original goal grew: to reach all the ethnic groups in the world. Simultaneously and not accidentally, missionary work around the world had exploded. The many Bible societies supported the work of churches and missions. Occasionally, the societies accommodated unique requests—all to get the Bible out.

Society members came from all Christian faiths. It was miraculous that the dedication to the Bible outweighed differences and transcended denominations and churches.

Churches and missions made requests to the Bible societies. Some requests were from churches with an established language. The society would print the Bible for them at little or no charge. A field representative would take up donations from those able to pay. This is how the Civil War soldiers in the 1860s received pocket Bibles.

After a foreign mission made a request, the society would accept the missionaries' translation. The society would print the Bibles and supply them to the mission—in the people's language.

Over time, the various Bible societies formalized their collaboration, known as the United Bible Society. The importance of these societies and their missionary partnerships must not be underestimated. This quiet work effectively provided the world with Bibles.

Today, there are **very few places in the world where the Bible is not available**, at least in part. The digital revolution now facilitates the goal: to reach all peoples of the world with the gospel message and a Bible. The centuries-long dream of many copyists and printers now lies well within reach.

IMPOSSIBLE TO DESTROY

In sum, from about 1800 to today, the Bible took a journey around the world—and it stayed. Today, a well-written, affordable Bible is available in every major language and in many dialects. Even some obscure languages have Bibles now. Missionaries, Bible translators, and Bible societies made great sacrifices. Their members and donors put their lives into this effort and have succeeded.

Burning the Bible and other such destruction was never successful in the past, but it is now utterly impossible.

THE OLD TESTAMENT

As previous chapters showed, the Israelites/Hebrews/Jews were and are **meticulous in their care of their Scripture**. They were, after all, the People of the Book. Over the centuries since the destruction of the Temple, they had set up special centers for the study and preservation of what Christians call the Old Testament. The Masoretic family of scribes, active from AD 600–900, are legendary for their meticulous copies of Scripture. So, we have confidence that we are reading as close to the accurate manuscripts, in Hebrew and in translation, of the Old Testament as it is possible to be.

The exciting find of the Dead Sea Scrolls in 1947 further shed light on the care of their Scripture by the Jews. These finds are dated to 250 BC, and show that transmission errors in the Old Testament were negligible.

Hebrew readers and scholars can now read the book of Isaiah from this find. The text of the Great Isaiah Scroll is visible on a facsimile in Museum of the Bible in Washington, DC.

Dead Sea Scrolls: Old Testament books found in clay jars in a cave near the Dead Sea. (Image courtesy of Facsimile Editions Ltd, 2025. https://facsimile-editions.com/dss/)

MORE POLISHING THE JEWEL

So vital is this methodology, it's important to review how the polishing occurs. By gathering and comparing manuscripts of ancient writings, a consolidated text of that work can be developed. This activity has rich history in Biblical studies as seen in chapter four.

> The point is: **modern textual criticism isn't mystical guesswork**. It's real science. Think of it as **documentary genealogy** or **literary detective work**. By it, scholars can trace the origin and history—the family tree—of various scrolls and codices. *(How We Got the Bible Made Easy.* Rose Publishing, 2020. Emphasis mine.)

As stated previously, the term "biblical criticism" has the connotation of subjecting the Bible to a negative process. "Biblical analysis" is a better term. Most of the genuine scholars who work in this field devote themselves to the Scripture and to making the best Greek New Testament possible.

To me, they would have to be devoted. The incredibly detailed effort requires years of education, the right temperament and the dedication of love—rare indeed.

Such analysis has its roots in antiquity. Even Homer's *Iliad* and *Odyssey* were analyzed this way by the ancient Greeks.

But in 1850 and beyond, the tools available to scholars greatly increased. As seen above, more manuscripts of ancient origin became available. And the goals changed. For many years, the goal was to discover the words from the original New Testament. Now making the best Greek version from which to make the best translation is the goal. Today, we have reached that goal in many ways. But the task continues.

How is this done? What is the process? Let's look at a big question regarding the end of Mark.

Some biblical analysts think Mark 16:9–20 was added to Mark at a later date

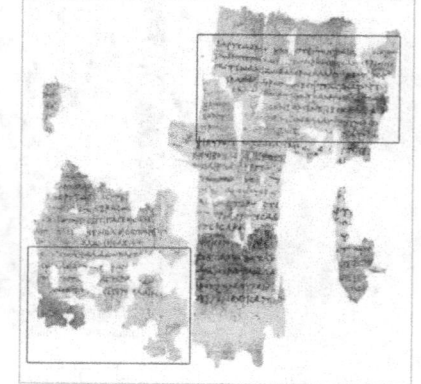

Two papyri of Homer's Iliad, one thousand years apart. (Graeme D. Bird, *Multitextuality in the Homeric Iliad: The Witness of the Ptolemaic Papyri.* Center for Hellenic Studies, 2010.)

and is therefore not original. Two of the three Witnesses above contain the book of Mark but **not Mark 16:9-20**. Yet other ancient codices do contain 16:9–20. So, what to do?

The solution for most Bible critics is to include the questionable section with a footnote, if there is enough precedent or evidence. For example, the New International Version states: "The most reliable early manuscripts and other ancient witnesses do not have Mark 16:9–20." Another approach is to put the questionable word, phrase, or section in a footnote as an alternative reading. Perhaps in the future, more light can be shed on such sections; manuscripts yet undiscovered may lay the question to rest.

So, **polishing this precious jewel is in a good place**, and more polishing may happen in the future given new findings and new techniques.

THE BIBLE GOES TO THE MOON AND BEYOND

In 1971. on the Apollo 15 mission, David Scott took the New Testament to the Moon with him and left it there. Presented to him by Saint Christopher Episcopal Church, this Bible appears in a photo of his lunar rover, visible on the dashboard.

In addition, many microfilm copies of the Bible went to the moon and back, which were auctioned or given away. Apollo Prayer League and Rev. Mark M. Stout supported this microfilm project.

Apollo 15 astronaut Dave Scott left a Bible on his lunar rover in 1971. (David Frohman. "The Story of the First Lunar Bible." David Frohman, 2018. https://lunarbible.com/)

Several astronauts have read Bible passages while they beheld the majestic universe from their perch in space. The space travelers themselves signify God's blessing on the accomplishments of mankind.

What about beyond? Voyager 1 and 2 were launched in 1977 and now are in interstellar space. We would expect the payload to contain the Bible. But neither the Bible nor any other religious items are listed aboard either Voyager in the public list of items. This is curious, since a religious impulse in humankind is well documented by anthropologists in all human activity from the most ancient of times until today.

But the Voyagers do contain, among many other things on the Golden Record, a photo of a man eating ice cream, a woman shopping in a grocery store, and fifty-five greetings to aliens in many modern and ancient languages—just in

Microfilm Bible to the moon and back. (David Frohman. "The Story of the First Lunar Bible." David Frohman, 2018. https://lunarbible.com/)

case. Add to these various sounds (man-made and natural), nature photos, a greeting and speech from President Jimmy Carter, and a brain-wave scan, and you get the picture.

Maybe the Bible would be an embarrassing record of the history of humanity when revealed to any aliens—what with all the violence, sin, and rebellion against our Creator it contains. But perhaps other beings already know it.

FINIS

ACKNOWLEDGMENTS

Whereas in antiquity biblical writers wrote in group settings, the process did change over time. Remember Hawthorne in his attic?

In more recent times, individuals could write alone, but the myth that they were an island unto themselves is obvious today. No one writes alone, really! We all have editors to thank—those pesky but necessary ones!

Test Readers (you know who you are) can't be thanked enough. The support of my family and friends is invaluable. Without such people we might just give up.

For this book, the hundreds (maybe even thousands) of contributors both past and current came to me in books, magazines, online searches, and other written and oral sources.

Thanks is such a shallow word; deep gratitude comes closer to expressing what I feel for all these contributions.

Appendix: Museum of the Bible

In Washington, DC., an amazing place awaits your perusal: Museum of the Bible. Here you can see a chronological collection of Bibles and other artifacts—and much more.

Exterior of Museum of the Bible, Washington, DC. *(Image courtesy of Museum of the Bible)*

Among these, you'll find a fine full-size model of a Gutenberg press, sometimes accompanied by a press worker. A full facsimile of the Great Isaiah Scroll is visible in the exhibit about the Dead Sea Scrolls. Whether you are walking through a replica of a town in Jesus' day, or enjoying a temporary exhibit among the rotating halls, Museum of the Bible is much more than a quick tour. I have been there several times and a two-day visit is not enough!

Tel Dan Stele with inscription of King David *(Image: special lecture promotion from Museum of the Bible)*

Exhibit of typical village in Jesus' time, such as Nazareth *(from MuseumoftheBible.org)*

Appendix: Word Topiary

The following *Tree of Biblical Figures* is from a precious 1931 book by William P. Pearce, titled *The World's Best Book and the Best Book for the World.*

When this word topiary was produced, no computers existed to count the words. All were hand-counted by someone of amazing skill and dedication.

The version of the Bible used for this unique work is unknown. However, the Revised Version of 1881 is the most likely candidate. Enjoy these unusual and intriguing Bible facts.

The Tree of Biblical Figures

THE
Bible con-
tains 3,566,480
letters, 810,697 words,
31,175 verses, 1,189 chapters,
and 66 books; the longest chapter is the 119th psalm; the shortest
and middle chapter is the 117th
psalm; the middle verse is the 8th
of the 118th psalm. The longest name
is in the 8th chapter of Isaiah. The word
and occurs 46,627 times. The 37th chapter of Isaiah and the 19th chapter of the 2d
book of Kings are alike. The longest verse
is the 9th of the 8th chapter of Esther; the
shortest, the 35th of the 11th chapter of
John. The 21st verse of the 7th chapter of
Ezra is the only one of the entire collection which contains every letter of the
alphabet but J. The word Lord, or
its equivalent, JEHOVAH, occurs 7,698 times in the
Old Testament; or,
to be more exact,
the word
LORD oc-
curs 1,853
times, and
the word
JEHOVAH
5,845 times. The word God does
not occur in the book of Esther;
BUT THERE IS WISDOM,
KNOWLEDGE, HOLINESS,
AND LOVE IN EVERY
CHAPTER OF THE ENTIRE WORK.

(10)

Word Topiary by William P. Pearce

Appendix: The One Year Bible

If I could help you read the Bible, would you read it?

Have you ever tried to read all the way through, start to finish, Genesis to Revelation? To call it a daunting task is an understatement. Most people get bogged down in lists of names and dietary laws, which had great purpose when given but are not easy to read, or even interesting to most.

But easier ways are available using **The One Year Bible**. It arranges the entire Bible into daily portions, one each from the Old and New testaments as well as Psalms and Proverbs. When you finish, you will have read the Bible cover to cover, start to finish, Genesis to Revelation! Below is an image directly from its introduction.

The One Year Bible comes in many translations and versions, from the vintage King James Version to the more up-to-date New International Version (NIV) and more in between. I like the NIV, which is a thought-for-thought translation, using the most current scholarship. The Living Bible is a paraphrase that is easy to read.

If you prefer the traditional, the New King James Version is both easier to read than the original King James and updated in scholarship.

There are times of life that we need to follow the dates with discipline, as a way of confirming our hunger. After repeating the discipline for years now, I do not adhere religiously to the dates. I mark January 1 as **my day one** on my own schedule. By reading the daily allotments in sequence, there's liberty to think slowly over each one. This way, I have successfully read through the Bible multiple times.

Some people are trained that the Bible is so holy you shouldn't alter it in any way. I agree it is holy, and for that reason I take notes which helps me interact with what the Bible says. With a pen that doesn't bleed through, I circle, underline, draw connections between verses, and write in the margin. Then when I finish the Bible, I get a new *The One Year Bible* and start over with a clean page.

And hey! You can get more points on *Jeopardy* if you know the Bible.

Ways to Use
THE ONE YEAR BIBLE

The One Year Bible is divided into daily readings. For each day there is a portion of the Old Testament, the New Testament, Psalms, and Proverbs. The four separate daily readings are grouped on consecutive pages, giving freshness and diversity to each day's reading. This also makes it easy to use *The One Year Bible* in a variety of ways.

The One Year Bible has led millions of readers through the Bible in one year. Its arrangement, however, is equally useful for guiding a reader through the Bible in two, or even three, years. If you feel too rushed or want to spend more time on each day's selections, here are a few other suggested reading plans:

The Revised One-Year Plan. Schedule some time in both the morning and evening. Then read the New Testament and Psalms selections in the morning and the Old Testament and Proverbs selections in the evening.

The Two-Year Plan. During the first year, just read the Old Testament and Proverbs selections. Then during the second year, read the selections from the New Testament and Psalms.

The Three-Year Plan. Read the Old Testament selection the first year, the New Testament selection the second year, and the Psalms and Proverbs selections during the third year.

Words of Praise and Wisdom in One Year. Read the Psalms and Proverbs selections for each day. This will take you through the Psalms twice and Proverbs once during the year, giving you words of praise and wisdom to live by each day.

You need not limit yourself to these suggested plans. The arrangement of *The One Year Bible* makes it easy to devise any number of Bible reading plans to meet your particular needs.

General Bibliography

Arnold, John H. *History: A Very Short Introduction*. Oxford University Press, 2000.

Barclay, William. *The Making of the Bible*. Lutterworth Press, 1961.

Barton, John. *A History of the Bible: The Story of the World's Most Influential Book*. Viking, 2019.

Barton, John. *How the Bible Came to Be*. Westminster John Knox Press, 1997.

Collins, Francis S. *The Language of God: A Scientist Presents Evidence for Belief*. Free Press, 2006.

Comfort, Philip Wesley and F. F. Bruce, editors. *The Origin of the Bible*. Tyndale House Ministries, 1992.

De Hamel, Christopher. *The Book: A History of the Bible*. Phaidon Press Ltd., 2016.

How Was the Bible Written? https://www.truthnet.org/Bible-Origins. Author and date unknown.

Huber, Robert V. and Stephen M. Miller. *The One-Stop History of the Bible*. Lion Hudson, 2016.

Jeffrey, David Lyle. *People of the Book: Christian Identity and Literary Culture*. Wm. B. Eerdmans Publishing Co., 1996.

Jones, Timothy Paul. *How We Got the Bible*. Rose Publishing LLC, 2015.

Keller, Werner. *The Bible as History*. Barnes & Noble Books, 1956.

Kenyon, Frederic G. *Our Bible and the Ancient Manuscripts: Being a History of the Text and Its Translations*. Kessinger Publishing, 2021.

Kenyon, Frederic G. *Our Bible and the Ancient Manuscripts*. Eyre & Spottiswoode, 1896.

Kenyon, Frederic G. *The Story of the Bible*. Wm. B. Eerdmans Publishing Co., 1967.

Lightfoot, Neil R. *How We Got the Bible*. Baker Book House, 1963.

Marty, William H. *The Whole Bible Story: Everything That Happens in the Bible in Plain English*. Bethany House Publishers, 2011.

Miller, Stephen M. and Robert V. Huber. *The Bible: A History: The Making and Impact of the Bible*. Good Books, 2004.

Miller, Stephen M. *The Complete Guide to the Bible*. Barbour Publishing, 2007.

Pearce, William P. *The World's Best Book and the Best Book for the World*. Pacific Press Publishing Assoc., 1931.

Reeves, Ryan M. and Charles E. Hill. *Know How We Got Our Bible*. Zondervan Publishers, 2018.

Schiffman, Lawrence H. and Jerry Pattengale, editors. *The World's Greatest Book: The Story of How the Bible Came to Be*. Worthy Books, 2017.

Schmid, Konrad and Jens Schröter. *The Making of the Bible: From the First Fragments to Sacred Scripture*. Harvard University Press, 2021.

Stone, Larry. *The Story of the Bible: The Fascinating History of Its Writing, Translation and Effect on Civilization*. Thomas Nelson, 2010.

Süe, Eugène. *The Pocket Bible or Christian the Printer: A Tale of the Sixteenth Century*. Reprint, 1842.

Wegnet, Paul D. *The Journey from Texts to Translations: The Origin and Development of the Bible*. Bridgepoint Books, 1999.

Willem Van Loon, Hendrik. *The Story of the Bible*. Garden City Publishing Co. Inc., 1923.

Woods, Len, contributor. *How We Got the Bible Made Easy*. Rose Publishing LLC, 2020.

Chapter 1 Bibliography

Carr, David M. *Writing on the Tablet of the Heart: Origins of Scripture and Literature*. Oxford University Press, 2005.

Charles River Editors. *The Ancient Canaanites: The History of the Civilizations That Lived in Canaan Before the Israelites*. Charles River Editors, 2016.

Chomsky, William. *Hebrew: The Eternal Language*. The Jewish Publication Society of America, 1957.

Davies, Philip R. and Thomas Römer, editors. *Writing the Bible: Scribes, Scribalism and Script*. Routledge, 2014.

Dever, William G. *Who Were the Early Israelites: And Where Did They Come From?* William B. Eerdmans Publishing Co., 2003.

Ford, Clayton Howard. *Who Really Wrote the Bible? A Response to the Documentary Hypothesis*. Self-Published, 2009.

Hamon, Bill. *Prophetic Scriptures Yet to Be Fulfilled: During the Third and Final Church Reformation*. Destiny Image Publishers, 2011.

Hamon, Bill. *Who Am I and Why Am I Here? Eight Reasons God Created the Human Race*. Destiny Image Publishers, 2005.

Kelly, Lynne. *The Memory Code: The Secrets of Stonehenge, Easter Island and Other Ancient Monuments*. Pegasus Books, 2017.

Miller (II), Robert D. *Oral Tradition in Ancient Israel*. Cascade Books, 2011.

Morris, Henry M. *The Genesis Record: A Scientific & Devotional Commentary on the Book of Beginnings*. Baker Book House, 1976.

Sáenz-Badillos, Angel; John Elwolde, translator. *A History of the Hebrew Language*. Cambridge University Press, 1988.

Taylor, Charles V. "Who Wrote Genesis? Are the Toledoth Colophons?" *Journal of Creation,* no. 8 (1994): (2):204-211. https://creation.com/who-wrote-genesis-are-the-toledoth-colophons.

Van Der Toorn, Karel. *Scribal Culture and the Making of the Hebrew Bible*. Harvard University Press, 2007.

Chapter 2 Bibliography

Batey, Richard A. *Jesus & the Forgotten City: New Light on Sepphoris and the Urban World of Jesus.* Baker Book House, 1991.

Beckwith, Roger T. *The Old Testament Canon of the New Testament Church: And Its Background in Early Judaism.* Wipf & Stock, 1985.

Cahill, Thomas. *Desire of the Everlasting Hills: The World Before and After Jesus.* Anchor Books, 2001.

Cahill, Thomas. *The Gifts of the Jews: How a Tribe of Desert Nomads Changed the Way Everyone Thinks and Feels.* Nana A. Talese/Doubleday, 1998.

Carr, David M. *The Formation of the Hebrew Bible: A Reconstruction.* Oxford University Press, 2011.

Cline, Eric H. *Biblical Archaeology: A Very Short Introduction.* Oxford University Press, 2009.

Edersheim, Alfred. *The Bible History: Old Testament.* William B. Eerdmans Publishing Co., 1890.

Fiensy, David A. *Galilee in the Late Second Temple and Mishnaic Periods: Life, Culture, and Society.* Fortress Press, 2014.

Finkelstein, Israel and Neil Asher Silberman. *The Bible Unearthed: Archaeology's New Vision of Ancient Israel and the Origin of Its Sacred Texts.* Touchstone, 2002.

Goldingay, John. *Approaches to Old Testament Interpretation.* InterVarsity Press, 1981.

Grabbe, Lester L. *An Introduction to Second Temple Judaism: History and Religion of the Jews in the Time of Nehemiah, the Maccabees, Hillel and Jesus.* T&T Clark International, 2010.

Hiebert, Murray D. *100 Reasons to Trust Old Testament History.* Self-Published, 2005.

Hope-Haley, Amanda. *The Red-Haired Archaeologist: Digs Israel.* Harvest House Publishers, 2021.

Isbouts, Jean-Pierre and Bridget E. Hamilton, et al. *The Story of Jesus.* Meredith Corporation, 2016.

Keith, Chris. *Jesus' Literacy: Scribal Culture and the Teacher from Galilee.* Bloomsbury Publishing, 2011.

Keith, Chris. *The Gospels as Manuscript: An Early History of the Jesus Tradition as Material Artifact.* Oxford University Press, 2020.

Kitchen, K. A. *On the Reliability of the Old Testament.* Wm. B. Eerdmans Publishing Co., 2003.

Leiman, Sid Z. *The Canonization of Hebrew Scripture: The Talmudic and Midrashic Evidence.* The Connecticut Academy of Arts & Sciences, 1991.

Margolis, Max Leopold. *The Hebrew Scriptures in the Making.* Jewish Publication Society of America, 1922.

Mears, Henrietta. *A Look at the Old Testament: An Abridged Survey of Genesis to Malachi.* Regal Books, 1967.

Schniedewind, William M. *Who Really Wrote the Bible: The Story of the Scribes.* Princeton University Press, 2024.

Chapter 3 Bibliography

Arlandson, James M. "Did Some Disciples Take Notes During Jesus' Ministry?" *Dr. Jim's Essential Bible Teaching.* https://drjimsebt.com/2022/04/18/8-did-some-disciples-take-notes-during-jesus-ministry.

Barnet, Peter and Nancy Wu. *The Cloisters: Medieval Art and Architecture.* Yale University Press, 2013.

Camillo Barone, "After centuries out of sight, the oldest surviving Hebrew Bible is making a permanent move to Israel." Forward.com, 2023. https://forward.com/news/563326/codex-sassoon-israel/)

Boynton, Susan, Editor. *The Practice of the Bible in the Middle Ages: Production, Reception, and Performance in Western Christianity.* Columbia University Press, 2011.

Bruce, F. F. *New Testament History.* Doubleday, 1971.

Bruce, F. F. *The Canon of Scripture.* InterVarsity Press, 1988.

Bruce, F. F. *The New Testament Documents: Are They Reliable?* InterVarsity Press, 1960.

Cahill, Thomas. *How the Irish Saved Civilization: The Untold Story of Ireland's Heroic Role from the Fall of Rome to the Rise of Medieval Europe.* Bantam Doubleday, 1995.

Coldstream, Nicola. *Medieval Architecture.* Oxford University Press, 2002.

De Hamel, Christopher. *Medieval Craftsmen: Scribes and Illuminators.* University of Toronto Press, 1994.

Graham, Henry, Rt. Rev. *Where We Got the Bible: Our Debt to the Catholic Church.* TAN Books, 1977.

Kruger, Michael J. *The Question of Canon: Challenging the Status Quo in the New Testament Debate.* InterVarsity Press, 2013.

Mantel, Hilary. *Bring Up the Bodies.* Fourth Estate, 2012.

Mantel, Hilary. *The Mirror & the Light.* Fourth Estate, 2020.

Mantel, Hilary. *Wolf Hall.* Fourth Estate, 2009.

Metzger, Bruce M. I. *The Canon of the New Testament: Its Origin, Development and Significance.* Clarendon Press, 1987.

Metzger, Bruce M. *The Text of the New Testament: Its Transmission, Corruption, and Restoration.* Oxford University Press, 1992.

Metzger, Bruce M. and Bart D. Ehrman. *The Text of the New Testament: Its Transmission, Corruption, and Restoration.* Oxford University Press, 1992.

Morris, Stephen. *The Early Eastern Orthodox Church: A History, AD 60–1453.* McFarland & Co. Publishers, 2018.

Nelson, Jinty and Damien Kempf, editors. *Reading the Bible in the Middle Ages.* Bloomsbury Publishing, 2015.

Norman, Jeremy. "Transitional Phases in the Form and Function of the Book before Gutenberg: The Transition from Oral to Written Culture." *History of Information.* Jeremy Norman & Co., Inc., 21 Aug. 2011. Web. 05 Mar. 2016. http://www.historyofinformation.com/narrative/oral-to-written-culture.php.

Oman, Charles. *The Dark Ages: 476–918.* Ergodebooks, 1898.

Rummel, Erika. "A Sixteenth Century Influencer: Getting to Know Erasmus." *Christian History,* Issue 145 (2022). Pages 6–10.

Sekules, Veronica. *Medieval Art.* Oxford University Press, 2001.

Smalley, Beryl. *The Study of the Bible in the Middle Ages*. University of Notre Dame Press, 1964.

Souter, Alexander. *The Text and Canon of the New Testament*. Chas. Scribner & Sons, 1913.

Tuchman, Barbara W. *A Distant Mirror: The Calamitous 14th Century*. Alfred A. Knopf, 1978.

Vince, Ronald W., editor. *A Companion to the Medieval Theatre*. Greenwood Press, 1989.

"Book of Hours." Wikimedia Foundation. June 19, 2025. wikipedia.org/wiki/Book_of_hours.

Wilson-Dickson, Andrew. *The Story of Christian Music: From Gregorian Chant to Black Gospel*. Lion Publishing, 2003.

York, Karen, editor. *The Bible Illuminated: How Art Brought the Bible to an Illiterate World*. Worthy Books, 2017.

CHAPTER 4 BIBLIOGRAPHY

Armstrong, Elizabeth. *Robert Estienne, Royal Print: An Historical Study of the Elder Stephanus*. Cambridge University Press, 1954.

Bauckham, Richard. *Jesus and the Eyewitnesses: The Gospels as Eyewitness Testimony*. Wm. B. Eerdmans Publishing Co., 2006.

Browne, George. *The History of the British and Foreign Bible Society: From Its Institution in 1804 to the Close of Its Jubilee in 1854*. Anatiposi Verlag, 2023.

Canton, William. *A History of the British and Foreign Bible Society*. John Murray, 1904.

Childress, Diana. *Johannes Gutenberg and the Printing Press*. Twenty-First Century Books, 2008.

Curtis, A. Kenneth. "How the King James Bible was Born." *Christian History,* Issue 100 (2011). Pages 4–15.

Fea, John. *The Bible Cause: A History of the American Bible Society*. Oxford University Press, 2016.

Freedman, Harry. *The Murderous History of Bible Translations: Power, Conflict, and the Quest for Meaning*. Bloomsbury Press, 2016.

Man, John. *The Gutenberg Revolution: How Printing Changed the Course of History*. Transworld Publishers, 2002.

Chapter 5 Bibliography

Bird, Graeme D. *Multitextuality in the Homeric Iliad: The Witness of the Ptolemaic Papyri*. Center for Hellenic Studies, 2010.

Green, Steve and Todd Hillard. *The Bible in America: What We Believe About the Most Important Book in Our History*. DustJacket Press, 2013.

Greenslade, S. L., editor. *The Cambridge History of the Bible: The West from the Reformation to the Present Day*. Cambridge University Press, 1963.

Mears, Henrietta. *A Look at the Old Testament: An Abridged Survey of Genesis to Malachi*. Regal Books, 1967.

Miller, Glenn T. *Piety and Profession: American Protestant Theological Education, 1870–1970*. Wm. B. Eerdmans Publishing Co., 2007.

Roberts, Mark D. *Unmasking the Jesus Seminar*. 2005: https://www.patheos.com/blogs/mark-droberts/series/unmasking-the-jesus-seminar.

WHAT PASTORS ARE SAYING

"Wow!" is all I can say to this book! The way it was approached and thought out! This is impactful, and I believe each person who reads this can honestly say "YES" to the Bible! *Blake Pryor, pastor, Heritage Church of Freeport FL*

This excellent read is fun and fascinating and is filled with great biblical insights. The title speaks for itself. *The Bible: A Pack Of Lies—Or God's Honest Truth?* both reveals hidden facts and brings clarity about the origin of the Bible. DD Renfroe condenses into 100 pages her exhaustive study of an eight-page bibliography, and reveals many reasons to believe that the Bible is truly God's honest truth. Maybe you are a student expanding your knowledge of the Bible, or maybe you are a new or longtime believer in Christ. This book will bless you and expand your knowledge about Scripture's roots. *David & Allie Allen, pastors, New Covenant Church, Thomasville GA*

DD Renfroe's small volume covers the history about the Bible without getting bogged down in details. She writes with confidence that if people are given an overview of the Bible's history, they will appreciate it much more. Her deep confidence in the integrity and trustworthiness of the Bible is contagious and may open eyes and hearts to the Divine Author behind the human authors and preservers of the Bible. I recommend the book as a support to embrace the Bible as the word of God revealing God's Son, Jesus Christ, the Savior of the world and of each person who trusts in him. **Judson I. Stone, pastor and author of historical biographies *A Modest but Crucial Hero: The Life and Legacy of Rev. George E. Stone (1873-1899)*, and *Last Chapter of the Greatest Generation***

What if the Bible isn't a dusty book of legends—but a living record with roots deeper and truer than we've dared imagine? In *The Bible: A Pack of Lies—or God's Honest Truth?* D.D. Renfroe embarks on a personal investigation that became a passion project—unearthing the origins, transmission, and lasting integrity of Scripture across thousands of years. From ancient oral traditions and carved memory-staffs to the revolutionary invention of writing and the scribes who preserved God's words, this book brings fresh insight into how the Bible came to be—and why it still matters.

With the heart of a seeker and the mind of a researcher, Renfroe confronts cultural skepticism head-on, inviting readers to wrestle with evidence, history, and faith. Whether you're a curious skeptic, a new believer, or someone wearied by modern cynicism, this book offers a compelling case for the Bible's authenticity—not through blind belief, but through an honest, hope-filled journey of discovery. Because in a world full of noise, truth still speaks. ***David V. Holland, pastor and author of Light Slipping Through the Chaos: Finding The Real Story Behind Christmas***

WHAT AUTHORS AND
INFLUENCERS ARE SAYING

THE BYLINE OF THIS BOOK SAYS IT ALL! EVERYTHING HINGES ON where we spend eternity, so it is absolutely critical to do a deep dive into the Word of God and closely read every single word. This book by DD Renfroe shows the Bible's rich history with descriptive timelines, detailed maps, and distinct photos. My faith was again affirmed: the Bible really is God's Honest Truth! Her easy book is a must for every adult AND teen in America! *Tina Griffin, host of The Counter Culture Mom Show*

DD Renfroe's book confronts the challenge on its cover—Is the Bible true or not?—and answers it with persuasive, well-reasoned clarity. What sets this book apart is the absence of sentimental assurances; instead, she walks a reader through specific evidence for Scripture's credibility, and dismantles common myths for disdaining it.

She highlights the remarkable consistency of biblical manuscripts, copied with extreme accuracy across centuries—refuting the popular claim that the Bible has been "changed and re-changed" beyond recognition. Renfroe demonstrates how archaeological discoveries, once thought to contradict Scripture, repeatedly confirm it—from ancient cities to cultural practices in the Old Testament. Using fulfilled prophecy, Renfroe shows the orchestration that only a sovereign God could exert.

All this, DD Renfroe weaves into an accessible narrative that is intellectually satisfying, which guides any reader to see that the Bible, far from a mythological anthology, is a historically grounded, Spirit-breathed revelation.

By the end of the book, the reader is left with a clear sense that Scripture is trustworthy—not merely because faith affirms it, but because evidence supports it. Renfroe has crafted a compelling tool for both believers seeking confidence and skeptics seeking truth. ***Gerald McGlothlin, special guests publicist***

Reading this book was like sitting with a trusted friend to explore a topic dear to my heart. Through her depth of study and research, DD Renfroe teaches fascinating Bible history and masterfully presents the Scripture as a lifeline and a treasure. You will highly value this book and probably read it more than once. I loved reading your book, DD, and was sad to reach the final page. Bravo. This is a treasure! ***Dave & Linda Roeder, authors of Uprighting Relationships, leaders of Restoring the Foundations ministry***

DD Renfroe presents interesting and unique facts about the authenticity of the Bible, and sheds new light on how the Bible came into our present-day hands. As a history buff myself, I find Renfroe's research fascinating. This is surely a must-read book for anyone curious about how we acquired our Bibles today. ***Marilyn Turk, award-winning author of historical fiction and devotions***

This book deals with the writing and transmission of the books of the Bible. It includes many interesting and thought-provoking ideas, and much data on what the manuscripts went through during the course of history. Also given are good reasons to reject the Documentary Hypothesis. Overall, it's a helpful read for those who love the Bible, or for those who are skeptical about it. ***Harry Buerer, author, Following Christ: Rediscovering the Jewish Faith of Jesus***

DD Renfroe's book well defends the authenticity of the Bible from an historical perspective. Believers treated the Old and New Testaments with wonderful respect through the ages. I was glad she described the ancient manuscript discoveries and some of the many archeological finds showing that the Bible has not changed significantly over the centuries.

Reading the Bible, I've found a consistency of revelation although its authors span years and locations, because they were all inspired by the Holy Spirit making it a true book. Years ago, I got bogged down in Numbers and stopped reading the Bible. Finally I invited Jesus in, to eat the words with me like bread (Rev. 3:20). Praise God, the words became more alive to me because it is a supernatural Book. Believers have the privilege of a supernatural Holy Spirit to help us understand it. *Nancy Salvador, author of the two-volume Jesus the Bridge*

The Bible is, without question, the most prestigious and influential of all writings. In this book, DD Renfroe breaks down the history behind its most remarkable teachings, all in a clear and meaningful way. 1850 to the present stood out to me the most. Renfroe shows how responses to the Bible split in two directions: one group carried the true Word across the world, while the other distorted scripture and used it for the wrong reasons.

What moved me most was how people in the Civil War kept the Bible close to their heart—not just for guidance, but for protection. Those small Bibles actually stopped bullets that were meant to take someone's life. Renfroe's book reminds you powerfully what the Bible has been to people throughout history: light, truth, and sometimes even a shield. *Lawrence Philip, author of How to Become Your Superhero Self*

DD Renfroe's book *The Bible: A Pack of Lies—or God's Honest Truth?* is a compelling argument for the Word of God as an actual historical book. She writes for those whose academic mindset promotes disbelief in God. Each page in this short book chips away at that stronghold of unbelief, and causes the reader to realize that the Bible is real—not concocted by individuals with wild and crazy imaginations. May every intellectually intransigent person, everyone with a heart of stone, receive the Truth of God's Word. Your hunger will be ignited through every historical fact revealed in DD's writing. *Stacey Scott, deliverance minister, Georgia & Florida*

The Bible: A Pack of Lies—Or God's Honest Truth is a sweeping, faith-affirming journey through the remarkable history of God's Word—how it was written, preserved, cherished, and passed down through generations. Blending engaging storytelling with historical insight, this richly detailed account traces how Scripture endured through centuries of conflict, exile, and cultural upheaval.

With a historian's precision and a believer's heart, the author illuminates the human devotion and divine providence that kept Scripture alive and why those efforts matter profoundly today. Both informative and inspirational, *The Bible: A Pack of Lies—Or God's Honest Truth* reminds us that the Bible was not merely written—it was *lived, guarded, and loved* by those who refused to let the Word of the Lord fade from the hearts of His people.

Yet *The Bible: A Pack of Lies—Or God's Honest Truth* is more than history. It is a personal invitation. The author reminds readers why the Bible still matters: If it is real and true, then it reveals our lives and our eternal destiny. That challenge, simple yet profound, turns the book from an academic exploration into a personal encounter with the living Word.

Beautifully written, deeply researched, and spiritually stirring, *The Bible: A Pack of Lies—Or God's Honest Truth* will deepen your appreciation for the miracle of preservation that carried God's Word across millennia and invite you to encounter that same living Word for yourself. ***Ellen Fannon, award-winning author of Save the Date and Love in the Wind.***

DD Renfroe brings alive the Bible and its validity in this compelling, relevant, and enlightening look at how it came to be. In coherent explanation, she presents the history of the Bible in layman's terms, without compromise on important details and arguments for and against. In a conversational voice, the author reviews the compiling of the sacred Scriptures through historically vetted sources. She goes behind the curtain and plainly shows the success of the Bible's existence. Even with her shrewd research, there's such an ease to reading it as if DD holds the reader's hand. She makes the case for the Bible's validity in a palatable, pure, and impertinent argument. This text will be beneficial to many curious, skeptical, and otherwise truth-hungry minds. ***Katie Dale, author, But Deliver Me from Crazy***

DD Renfroe invites readers on an inspiring journey through history, archaeology, and faith to uncover the undeniable truth of Scripture's authenticity. With a researcher's mind and a believer's heart, she combines deep investigative work with storytelling that makes ancient evidence come alive. This book is a powerful encouragement for skeptics, seekers, and saints alike. It will strengthen your faith and equip you to stand confidently on the foundation of God's Word."—***Susan***

Neal, RN, MBA, MHS award-winning author of 12 Ways to Age Gracefully

DD Renfroe offers us a short, thoughtful glimpse of the process that the Word of God has endured throughout time. She meticulously documents the ancient modes people used to preserve the record of God's interaction with mankind. She explores the transformation of these records forward into modern history into the Bible we have today. Most importantly, you see the preservation of the record and its integrity, through divinely inspired human commitment and effort.

Her detailed approach highlights that human beings were so moved by their interactions with the divine God Most High that they created and preserved an enduring record of them. Each person who encounters HIM can testify to these experiences which reveal God's Word, His heart, and His Presence in our midst.
Valerie K Kinsman, author, Mysteries of the Kingdom of God, Jesus the Giver, and God the Giver